AMERICA'S MANIFEST DESTINY
How History Haunts U.S. Conservation Leadership

First Edition

AMERICA'S MANIFEST DESTINY
How History Haunts U.S. Conservation Leadership

An
Essay

Thomas E. Loxley

Tache Works

First Edition

AMERICA'S MANIFEST DESTINY
How History Haunts U.S. Conservation Leadership

Thomas E. Loxley

Tache Works

A special educational outreach publisher.
All rights are reserved. Address comments
to: Thomas Loxley, 680 Canal St.-No. 402,
Beaver, PA 15009. All feedback is welcome.

Manufactured in United States of America
ISBN: 9781733743051

Dewey Decimal Classification:
190 Modern Western Philosophy

BISAC Subject Codes:
HIS049000 HISTORY/Essays
POL045000 POLITICAL SCIENCE/Colonialism & Post-Colonialism
SCI092000 SCIENCE/Global Warming & Climate Change
SOC026000 SOCIAL SCIENCE/Sociology/General

Dedication

This work is dedicated to all those young people around the world who bravely stood up to demand that world leaders do something, right now, about global warming and saving our planet Earth.

TABLE OF CONTENTS

SUMMARY

America has seen a destructive politicization of its scientific concerns dealing with critical issues such as energy and the environment. This has represented a desire by some powerful special interests to restrict technological evolution so that it only perpetuated their dominating position. Aggressive lobbying obstructed fair competition and restricted any government support to their selfish benefit. Their power to actually control this situation has undermined its democracy and represents a growing national dysfunction that is dangerously affecting America's role in the world. The fundamental roots of this dilemma are traced to a relentless perpetuation of Manifest Destiny, the philosophy which was the driving force in colonial America. This exploitive psychological addiction has proven to be impossible to control. It is producing a pervasive national hypocrisy that defiles any hope of being a rational democracy. Study of our human population growth, resource depletion, consumptive lifestyles and leadership demands illustrates today's desperate need for a dynamic new renaissance in global altruism.

INTRODUCTION

Independent scientists, like myself, have long been subjected to America's changing national priorities regarding endeavors like space exploration, oceanic development, environmental protection and energy conservation. Many personal careers and valuable developments have clearly been lost in this utterly senseless shuffle, due to the destructive nature of America's political and industrial evolution.

My engineering career began with the U.S. Navy in 1961 in the midst of the Cold War with the former Soviet Union. They say that truth itself is the first casualty in any war, and this era saw an enormous growth in propaganda and disinformation programs of all sorts. American leadership now seems to have been vastly undermined by all of this insidious activity. Many now wonder if it is even possible to ever correct today's dysfunctional USA. The basic social cohesion that is needed to deal with any major problem, no longer seems to exist.

Progress invariably demands that we resist the personal temptation to take refuge from changing ideas in any form of dogmatism or denial. Change is constantly occurring all around us and change itself is the primary constant in life. Just how we deal with this fact is the final measure of our intelligence and integrity. Many scientists used to believe that

1

the natural changes in our environment all occurred very gradually. In fields such as geology, the Earth's sedimentary layers were seen as being deposited over many long eons of time. Only recently have catastrophic, destabilizing and cyclical phenomena been seen as playing major roles in punctuating Earth's evolution.[1] We are all now being forced to live together in an increasingly crowded world, where our own human population growth is all too often likened to that of some malignant disease.

Many historic empires collapsed far faster than anyone had anticipated. The responsible citizens in our own 'alleged' democracy now have an abiding obligation to confront the critical issues in society, before it then sinks into some truly monstrous tyranny. That decline is now often feared to be well underway. A great flood of confusing facts, lies and nonsense now seems to obstruct the objective resolution of most any problem. Highly paid media commentators are exploiting the public vulnerability to sensational propaganda just to boost their audience ratings and enormous pay checks. This essay is my own personal attempt to analyze the openly available information in order to draw some hopefully meaningful conclusions. Unless they are specifically attributed, all of the various interpretations, opinions and speculations expressed are strictly my own.

HUMAN POPULATION EXPLOSION

The Earth's human population was under 1-billion (10^9) prior to 1850, Figure 1.[2] Our population explosion then coincided with the industrial revolution. The human population reached 6-billion in 1999, 7-billion in 2012 and 8-billion in 2022.[3] How will this then affect our future generations? Children that most parents appear to love. How will those children then respond when they fully realize our irresponsibility in assuring their personal future? The growth seen in the human population clearly parallels the growth in all of the societal ills and stresses that are now undermining our daily lives. This dilemma is utterly all encompassing and defies any self-serving political or religious rationalizations.

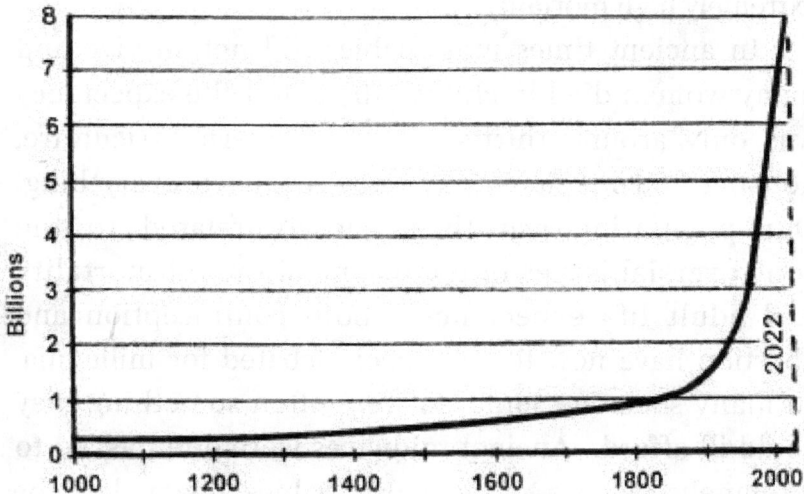

Figure 1: Historic growth of the human population.

It is believed that many of our current problems are a natural byproduct of our own biological evolution. Earth's history has been plagued by catastrophic events where only the most aggressive and procreative species then survived.[4] Such disasters have caused multiple mass extinctions of many lifeforms on Earth. The supervolcanic eruption of Sumatra's Toba Caldera, some 74,000 years ago, almost wiped out all of humanity.[5] This was far larger than Indonesia's Mount Krakatoa eruption, believed to cause the Dark Age in the year 535.[6] Somehow, surviving pockets of humanity were able to breed rapidly enough to sustain the species. Natural selection then favored the survival of those individuals having the greatest fertility and aggressive sexuality.[7] This frenetic procreation didn't cause many problems in the former population, due to its extremely high mortality.

In ancient times most babies did not survive and many women died in childbirth. Adult life expectancy was only around thirty years.[8] Modern agriculture, housing and medicine have now changed everything. Our population growth is clearly related to the controversial issues of birth control, infant mortality and adult life expectancy. Both contraception and abortion have now literally been debated for millennia. In many societies, children were often something they could ill afford. Ancient midwives were often asked to humanely dispose of newborn babies deemed to be unfit or unwanted. Such decisions were well rooted in the extremely harsh realities of most human existence. The righteous indignation of some today, who are infinitely better off, can only please their own religious vanity at the expense of those less fortunate. Major advances have now been made in birth control as well as in the monitoring and care of any pregnancy.

Many seem to be bent on saving every fetus, no matter how premature, compromised, or jeopardized their future or the mother's health may be. Decisions formerly made in private, by families and midwives, are being commandeered by politicians or delegated to hospital corporations that only seem interested in their own vain power or profitability. They seem unconcerned with the burden to the family or society, and often only seem to exploit any religious dogma benefiting their vanity or greed. Similar arguments apply to the medical tactics used to prolong the life of the elderly, who are often subject to some gruesome, hopeless and bankrupting ordeal.[9-10]

Aggressive procreation and modern technology have combined to yield our exploding population. Yet, it can be argued that every benefit in life has a price that must then be paid.[11-13] Since technology created the problem, more technology might solve it. Many believe anyone accepting the benefits of technology must then accept the full responsibility of dealing with its ramifications. This would then seem to demand the responsible conception and rearing of any children. It means a society is forever altered the moment that it accepts those benefits. No

5

wishful thinking can then bring the old ways back, unless they relinquish them. This will naturally then demand constant changes in the icons and perspectives in any community. It can only be hoped society will find reasonable ways to accept the new reality, without undermining their own cultural identity. Some nations have clearly accomplished this feat much better than others. Yet, many so-called adults still seem to be reluctant to objectively discuss any such personal matters.[14]

The world's regional population densities have varied with the local resources, climate and lifestyle, Table 1.[15] Between 1790 and 2000 the U.S. population increased eighteen fold. While America's population density seems low, compared to Bangladesh, one must realize that the average American now consumes about 50-times the natural resources as the Earth's average citizen. Indeed, many rich American families now literally devour more natural resources than many large foreign towns.

Table 1: Population density per square kilometer

Bangladesh	981	Pakistan	186	Turkey	86	Brazil	20
South Korea	488	Switzerland	176	Greece	81	Finland	17
Netherlands	471	Nigeria	139	Spain	80	New Zealand	14
India	347	China	137	Egypt	70	Argentina	14
Japan	335	Poland	127	Mexico	53	Saudi Arabia	10
U.K.	247	Denmark	127	Iran	41	Russia	9
Germany	237	Indonesia	125	U.S.A.	30	Australia	3
Italy	196	France	109	Sweden	22	Canada	2

Some Americans like to look at the present population density and declare there are still 3.2 hectares (8 acres) of land for everyone. However, such thinking neglects our need for a tolerable climate, natural resources and all of the amenities that we have come to demand. These now include food, water, sewage treatment, clothing, housing, health care, trash disposal, education, employment, recreation, transportation, communication, fire protection, law enforcement, national defense, government, etc. Few Americans can ever hope to have their own 3.2 hectares of personal space.

Konrad Lorenz warned us that as we crowded people ever closer together, we could expect them to exhibit increasingly destructive behavior.[16] Modern society has also introduced many disease multipliers in the form of changing climates, air and water pollution, accumulating waste, intense world trade, multiple sex partners, concentrated blood products, infected hospitals, reused hypodermic syringes, recycled air-conditioning, over crowded transportation, etc. Loren Eiseley's book, *The Firmament of Time,* foresaw our ever advancing technology yielding three fundamental human dilemmas: (1) A dynamic society that's increasingly difficult for people to adjust to; (2) Fascinating inventions that constantly divert our attention from learning how to live a well rounded life; and (3) A growing obsession with the material aspects of life that undermine development of any empathetic sense of responsibility.[17] All three of these concerns are then clearly exemplified in the self-serving credo of today's American predatory opportunists, who literally seem to dedicate their lives to taking wrongful advantage of everybody they can, and the easy one's more.

The premature deaths in America illustrate the present situation.[15] Suicide is now its eighth leading cause of death, third among Blacks. Some 30,000 Americans committed suicide in 2001 and 3-million young teenagers seriously considered it. Fully 15,000 murders occurred, with one-third going unsolved. Some 43,000 died in auto accidents, down due to improved automotive safety standards. Irresponsibly distracted drivers now effectively murder thousands of people annually, and cell-phone driving is the new Russian Roulette. One-third of auto fatalities are caused by drunk drivers, and 36 percent of age 16 to 19 deaths are due to auto accidents. Its 16-year-olds now have 8-times as many auto accidents as adults, with many fatalities attributed to the destructive peer pressure that adolescents aggressively exert on each other. More Americans now die from drug overdoses than auto accidents. Sixteen percent of the Americans in prison are mentally ill.[18-20] When Ronald Reagan closed America's mental institutions, to give wealthy taxpayers special relief, its mentally ill were literally dumped into the streets, prisons and senior citizen buildings. Despite all of its grand technical progress, the American lifestyle still seems to be dominated by their fundamental human appetites, fear and vanity. There appears to be little evidence of any intelligent reflection.[21-22] Overcome with all of the demands of modern life, everyone seems to now be constantly adjusting their priorities to suit their own comforts. The public reluctance to resolve any serious societal problems is often then attributed to willful blindness.[14]

U.S. politicians were encouraged to ignore the ugly facts of the Vietnam War in order to avoid any public examination of this very disturbing conflict. One that included half-a-million deserting American soldiers and up to some 2,000 assassinations, called fraggings, of American officers by their own men.[23] The war had been so aggressively driven by U.S. profiteering interests that one-third of its casualties resulted from faulty equipment, friendly fire and needless accidents. When war material failed to meet critical safety standards, American manufacturers aggressively pushed politicians to accept it anyway. This created situations where Americans at home, unknowingly, helped to maim and kill their own relatives serving in Vietnam. The big corporations then forced corrupt politicians to literally exempt them from any responsibility for their defective products, no matter how negligent they were. Now, many U.S. politicians seem perplexed when two-thirds of its potential voters cynically choose not to vote.[24-25] Indeed, many Americans now see the country as a sort of covert corporate fascist dictatorship. One that merely masquerades as a democracy in order to give its degenerate modern 'millionaire' politicians an illusion of legitimacy.

Many often see population growth as providing new customers or enlarging their special interest groups. Perhaps they would do better to consider the life of those living on the Philippine garbage dumps as a more relevant portrayal of many children's future.[26] While many deplored China's former harsh population controls, few can dispute that drastic measures were needed for it to ever become a modern industrial nation. Although Kerala, India, has progressively got its own population growth under control, it is unknown if the rest of the country will ever follow.[27] American sperm counts have dropped over 60 percent since 1932, forcing many couples to adopt foreign children or use radical new in vitro fertilization techniques. One-third of the world's population, and a quarter of America's own children, now go to bed hungry. Some 13.5-million Americans are known to be homeless for part of the year, and fully half-a-million undocumented immigrants live in squalid U.S. shantytowns, called colonias.[28]

What is the Earth's maximum sustainable human population?[29-31] This will naturally depend upon the arable land available. This has varied, depending on whether the Ice Ages were advancing or retreating.[32] Most estimates foolishly assume a perpetuation of present conditions. Some old Archer Daniels Midland Corporation advertisements talked of feeding a future world population of 10-billion (10^9). This clearly ignores all of the random catastrophes that are a natural part of Earth's history. Major environmental restoration may be needed just to perpetuate the current population. Assuming the best of conditions and diverse demands of different cultures, some question Earth's ability to even sustain over 2-billion people with any meaningful comfort and opportunity. The present population might conceivably be allowed to decline naturally until the population can regain some measure of control over their destiny. However, our ecological destruction of the planet may have now undermined our ability to properly support even that number.

The recent surges in international refugees from various wartorn states have now exposed an abject failure of the United Nations.[33] Many people now believe that it needs some innovative new tools to force countries to peacefully reconcile their internal problems in order to avoid them from imposing their desperate refugees on other countries This must deal with an array of political, economic and social concerns that are often rooted in regional disparities of wealth, power and privilege. I believe that the present United Nations partisan veto rights must be terminated and some automatic mechanisms created that can impose new leverage on any offenders.

NATURAL RESOURCE DEPLETION

European settlers started flooding into America some 500 years ago. Fleeing old feudal systems, many then saw the New World as a vast superabundant land where they might become princes of a grand new aristocracy.[34] When Native Americans proved to be incapable of effectively defending themselves, they were repeatedly pushed aside.[35] Their devastation then constituted a true Holocaust, where a population of over 25 million was reduced to only some 4 million descendants.[36-37] This relentlessly ugly process of systematic dispossession and extermination had frequently involved their cruel murder by diseases introduced from abroad. The 1830 Indian Removal Act then forcibly relocated the survivors to ever more barren lands west of the Mississippi River.[38] An event whose abject scale and utter meanness clearly resembled the awful death marches of World War II. Many settlers used African slaves, approved by the Roman Vatican, to work their vast land acquisitions. One-fifth died in transit, and half of the survivors were worked to death within ten years.[39] Manifest Destiny evolved as the American rationalization for all of this egregious behavior. It declared that any man who seized and held the property of 'lesser' men, so that it was put to 'better' use, had a God given right to do so.[40-41]

Like a horde of Machiavellian monarchs, they used brute force, money, legalisms and lies to get their way. Robber barons emerged who seized vast economic empires in timber, cotton, tobacco, corn, wheat, cattle, coal, silver, gold, steel, oil, railroads, ships, etc. They openly declared that whatever was 'good' for themselves was truly 'best' for the nation. Their flamboyant personal lifestyles and philosophies showed that they truly saw themselves as a uniquely new 'capitalistic' aristocracy.[42-45] And they all had lots of adoring fans who dreamed of exceeding even their wildest accomplishments. They then aggressively exploited any natural resources strictly for their immediate wealth. And when the easily accessed resource ran out, the despoiled lands were simply abandoned in the search for more easy pickings. Little respect was ever really given to any need to safeguard the environment or the local population.[46] Moreover, the philosophy of Manifest Destiny endures today in the subconscious thinking of many Americans. This can be seen in the persistence of irresponsible accounting practices that trivialize exploitable items like natural resources, environmental quality and the public welfare. Items that are truly essential to the survival of most any community.[47-48]

Natural resources can be basicly divided into organic and mineral substances. Organic resources include native game or plants that provide useful food or materials, plus domesticated animals and plants that may come from abroad. Fuels like wood, peat, or coal are often obtained from the ground surface. However, many valuable energy and mineral resources must be sought underground, utilizing specialized mining or drilling operations. The appropriate land is extremely critical to any industrial development, as is adequate fresh water. It is also important whether that water is readily available, from lakes or streams, or must be extracted from local springs or aquifers.[49]

Many industrial activities involve processing where chemical reagents are used and waste products are generated. While some waste may constitute usable byproducts, most must usually be disposed of in some responsible fashion.[50] It could be solid, liquid, or gaseous in nature and may react, chemically or biologically, with the local ecology. Manufactured items too are eventually discarded, and any solid waste then imposes segregation, collection and processing concerns. Waste water and sewage requires special storage, piping and processing. While such tasks may often seem onerous, they are the natural burdens associated with modern life. It would be highly irresponsible for anyone to consider themselves exempt from doing their part. Moreover, it's far easier and cheaper to handle such problems close to their source, rather than at some later stage.[46] Reducing packaging materials can cut the amount of trash produced.   Minimizing leakage and maximizing the combustion efficiency can reduce the environmental problems with utilizing any fuel.

The relations between society and its resources have changed greatly with the growing human population, especially in America.[51-52] In 500 years, many commercially viable biological resources have been destroyed and many lifeforms driven into extinction.[53] Water bodies that formerly teemed with salmon, trout, sturgeon and other species now lie barren and hopelessly fouled.   Many ocean fisheries were so recklessly exploited and polluted that they are no longer viable.[54]   Lifeless ocean deserts now exist. The millions of migrating passenger pigeons are gone, and its vast buffalo herds were wantonly murdered to destroy the basic lifestyle of Native Americans. Many living creatures have long since disappeared as their natural habitats were destroyed by human encroachment. Some powerful new ocean prospecting and sonar systems now threaten many valuable marine mammals, including any possible lifeforms that may have eluded discovery.[55]

Huge topsoil losses, due to wind and water erosion, have destroyed America's ability to raise many crops.   Large rural areas are now used for dumping domestic and industrial waste.[56] Factory farming has caused lost topsoil as well as soil and water contamination.   Its experts seem infatuated with modern technology, contending that only the biggest of farms are really economically viable.[57-58] Aggressive promotion of this self-serving corporate dogma has undermined political support for small farmers, who provide a valuable level of attention that the big corporate farmers simply cannot afford. In contrast, many Europeans live well on small farms. These produce more food per hectare than big American farmers, using half the energy and one quarter of the chemical fertilizer. Cooperative marketing and equipment sharing helped make such operations successful. Many now think that the very nature of American agriculture has yielded needless epidemics of diabetes, heart disease and colon cancer.[59]

American agriculture now seems to be controlled by a few huge corporate conglomerates, which aggressively shape national policies to then suit themselves.[57-58] This seems to defy common sense when they construct facilities to raise millions of hogs at a time in huge buildings, with all of their waste being dumped directly into giant lagoons.[60-61] Although the public health problems and the foul stench would surely appear problematic, these seem readily ignored by America's remote corporate profiteers and local politicians.[62] Much smaller operations caused problems in 1999, when Hurricane Floyd scattered rotting hog corpses over a huge area. Many now fear high tech insecticides have caused the present Colony Collapse Disorder that threatens the honeybees needed for plant polination.[63] Others

16

believe that such toxins may have also caused autism, asthma and other ailments.[64-66]

The overgrazing of many vulnerable pasture lands is another factor in causing increased soil erosion. This is especially true in America's federal grazing lands, where corporate ranchers have used political pressure to purchase unrestricted grazing rights at a small fraction of their true value. Some 1.2-million hectares (3-million acres) of arable land are lost annually to growing urban and suburban communities. Enormous areas of prime land have been despoiled by irresponsible and poorly regulated mining and drilling operations. Many seem to be designed so that when the easily exploited deposit runs out, the sham corporations declare bankruptcy to avoid the cost of land reclamation. Vast areas now lie criminally despoiled in ways that contaminate the local drinking water.[67-68] U.S. mining interests had aggressively lobbied to keep the acceptable level of arsenic, a major carcinogen, at 50 parts per billion (ppb), rather than the 10 ppb required in Europe. All mining operations are now being forced to exploit lower grade deposits. This has caused them to process ever larger volumes of raw material and the amount of waste generated to then skyrocket. Modern technology now offers equipment and explosives that can literally move mountains, causing monstrous devastation. America's growing production of household waste has driven the construction of enormous landfills.[69] New York City trash is now routinely being hauled by the trainload to a landfill in Ohio. America's organized criminals have now destroyed many beautiful rural areas by illegally dumping toxic industrial fluids and dangerously infected medical waste in valuable woodlands and along rural roadsides.

All these activities impacted watersheds vital to local drinking water. This is often compounded by the mixing of storm drainage with sewage systems, causing waterways to be polluted with raw sewage during heavy rains. Due to its toxic contamination, processed sewage has had very limited value as a fertilizer. The corporate political control of waste legislation has undermined the recycling of many materials. Burning has also been discouraged due to potential air pollution. High fuel consumption has led to leaky underground storage tanks and pipelines contaminating many valuable lands and fresh water sources.[70-71] Leakage of the gasoline additive MTBE (methyl-tertiary-butyl-ether) has contaminated many water wells, with no known way to ever clean up these vital aquifers. Many people now suffer severe water shortages, with their previous sources being exhausted or polluted. Some aquifers are now so low that it is no longer practical to pump the water out.

Its oil and gas deposits have also been aggressively exploited. New domestic oil and gas production requires expensive new production technology, drilling deeper new wells, or exploiting difficult offshore or Arctic deposits.[72-76] Many options represent increased environmental risks and expense. New tar sands and shale fracking operations incurr markedly increased costs, global warming effects and fearful transport explosions. Daily explosions now occur on all the aging natural gas pipelines crisscrossing America, yielding environmental damage that's estimated over $850-million a year.[77-78] Today's heavy shipping traffic has also come to represent a major threat to world waterways.

All of this human behavior has a political and psychological momentum that is very hard to reverse. Different national philosophies govern fuel prices in the U.S. and Europe, where they can be 3-times as high. This is due to provisions for dealing with the costs of highways, pollution, energy conservation, resource depletion and alternative transport.[79-81] Their socially responsible approach then contrasts sharply with the overbearing corporate influence that now controls many American policies. Industrial propaganda also routinely ignores any destructive aspects of their operations. Another dilemma lies in America's failure to honestly account for the natural resources expropriated from Native American lands. The U.S. Department of Interior has long been seen as being criminally incompetent in providing the full compensation that's rightfully due for these materials.[82]

19

MODERN CONSUMPTIVE LIVING

A nation's lifestyle is reflected in its per capita energy use, Table 2.[83] It is often noted that while the world's industrial nations comprise one-fifth of its population, they consume two-thirds of its resources and produce four-fifths of the pollution. And while Americans are 5 percent of its population, they've long used 25 percent of its oil and produced 25 percent of the carbon dioxide. Although it consumes about 40 percent of all the Earth's natural resources, others do a better job of saving energy. The Internet itself has been an unanticipated energy use. It consumes 8 percent of U.S. electrical power and could soon consume half of the electricity in the city of Seattle. When this is added to the demands for new construction and the upgrading of older buildings, it has pushed some power systems to their limits. This has resulted in low voltage brownouts and rolling type electrical blackouts. The U.S. capacity is becoming unable to meet demands, and new power plants often take fifteen years to build.

Table 2: Annual per capita energy use (megawatt-hours)

U.S.A.	91.0	New Zealand	51.1	Spain	37.7	Turkey	12.9
Finland	84.3	South Korea	50.7	Italy	36.5	Brazil	12.5
Sweden	67.3	Germany	49.1	Greece	31.5	Nigeria	9.1
Canada	66.9	Japan	47.2	Poland	27.7	Egypt	8.9
Australia	66.8	France	46.2	Iran	23.7	Indonesia	8.8
Saudi Arabia	65.2	U.K.	45.7	Argentina	18.4	India	6.0
Netherlands	58.5	Denmark	44.7	Mexico	17.9	Pakistan	5.3
Russia	51.6	Switzerland	43.4	China	13.3	Bangladesh	1.9

Much of America's dilemma lies in its destructive peer pressure, where people are compelled to measure their individual worth in increasing amounts of money and material possessions.[84] Many believe they will be failures if they aren't millionaires by forty. It is widely believed that MONEY is the only GOD that's truly worshiped in America. And until wanton and insatiable greed is seen as a psychiatric disease, such behavior is expected to continually get worse. Although they take eager advantage of any ancestral wealth, power, or prestige, few American families accept any moral responsibility for their ancestral wrongdoing. Justice Department Prosecutor, John Loftus, alleged President George W. Bush's trust fund, which financed his political career, was derived from his grandfather's financial service to Nazi Germany.[85]

Americans have seen all too many questionable changes in economic policies. These, often covert, maneuvers illustrate the fundamental hubris that was dramatically enhanced after World War II. A period then explored in the Kevin Phillips' book *Bad Money*.[86] America left the gold standard in 1971 and concern exists over the wisdom of having one nation's currency as the world's reserve currency. What might lie ahead for the U.S. dollar, when it is one of the world's biggest debtors? Will it then militarily compel everyone on Earth into perpetuating its international dominance? The political manipulation of unemployment, inflation, economic growth and productivity data is alarming.

U.S. politicians often tout low unemployment, compared to Europe, while hiding their statistical adjustments to make themselves look good and avoid dealing with many problems.[87] John F. Kennedy had launched this destructive process with a special committee that then revised its calculation. Many unemployed people nowadays go uncounted and the military are being used to inflate the total job holders. Bill Clinton altered black unemployment by dropping many city residents and discounting their actual poverty. Those people who run out of any temporary benefits, or have never worked full-time, now go uncounted.

Monthly Consumer Price Index (CPI) data track a bundle of prices that are supposed to reflect current living costs. Yet, politicians drop or adjust any components from housing, food and energy that might hinder their minimization of the inflation rate. Ronald Reagan introduced a nebulous new Owner Equivalent Rent to minimize rising housing costs. The adjusted inflation calculations were also reduced by employing substitutions, like hamburger for steak. Geometric weighting then also helped to cut costs. Bill Clinton's own hedonistic adjustments cut the CPI by then assuming modern technology, like air travel, somehow offered special benefits. George W. Bush added a whole new calculation procedure that was designed to reduce the inflation estimates. All of these steps kept down wages and Social Security benefits that would otherwise be up by over 70 percent.

America replaced the term Gross National Product in 1991 with Gross Domestic Product, due to its growing national debt. This allowed adjustments for starting up and closing businesses, and unfounded 'phantom' numbers for nebulous benefits, like free checking accounts. These steps alone represented some 15 percent of the GDP calculation in 2007.

Numerous U.S. failings are rooted in its reckless elimination or failure to enforce important economic regulations. Predatory lending, fraudulent financial derivatives and the bundling of good and bad mortgages for sale to unsuspecting investors was highly promoted. The national economy has also been greatly undermined by the many destructive mergers and acquisitions that have effectively destroyed any competition. Unregulated investment vehicles, like CDOs and swaps, and forced stock market fluctuations, due to computerized trading, have further undermined any respectable concept of commerce in the United States.[88]

Americans are seen as the world's worst litterbugs, producing twice as much trash as people in Germany.[69] While the average automotive gas consumption per mile declined abroad, it has often risen in America due to the popularity of gas guzzling types of vehicles. Many communities have no sidewalks, bicycle paths, or mass transit, forcing people to drive everywhere, often alone. America has almost as many registered vehicles as adults, with many families having up to three or more cars.[89] Teenagers routinely force their parents to buy them a car for their sixteenth birthday, inspite of all the dangers involved. Its societal problems are further compounded by the fact that one-fourth of U.S. alcoholic beverages are illegally consumed by very young children. And those starting before age 15 are considered 5-times more likely to become alcoholics as those starting at age 21. Half of its college students now indulge in binge drinking and it is feared that this generation could be seriously crippled by its alcohol and drug abuse.[90] Americans now literally consume half of all the illicit drugs that are used on Earth. This is expected to yield increasing numbers of children being born with expensive special needs. It is also feared to pose added potential dilemmas by allowing many impaired people to work at home, unsupervised, on the Internet.

America's delusional War-on-Drugs cannot hope to succeed if it fails to attack the fundamental roots of the problem. These are seen as the irresistible lure of easy money and the desperate need for people to escape the perceived misery of their lives. These are the natural byproducts of modern American life. The need for personal satisfaction should require serious attention in a modern democracy. Personal income tax returns could be made public, via the Internet, so local peer pressure might discourage wrongful activity.[91] The drug war is perpetuating large bureaucratic and corporate empires that now consume vast financial resources that are desperately needed elsewhere. Of 8-million people imprisoned on Earth, 2.4-million are Americans.[18-20]

24

One-percent of U.S. adults are now behind bars. As the world's premier prison capital, Americans are being jailed at a rate over 7-times that in China. California now spends more money on prisons than universities and the average annual cost per prisoner runs around $30,000. Although whites now consume some 5-times the illicit drugs, blacks are 7-times more likely to go to prison.[92] A black man born today has a one-in-three chance of going to jail at sometime in their lives. This has created a growing belief that the phony War on Drugs has long been corrupted to serve racial bigotry. Meanwhile, its profiteering prison corporations are constantly lobbying for the incarceration of ever more Americans.

It can well be argued that many of America's deteriorating social conditions are directly related to the dynamic growth of its personal materialism, which is now often described as conspicuous consumption. America has ten-times the retail selling space per capita as Britain. Hollywood and the media are often seen as popularizing many irresponsible behaviors. They have played a vital role in manipulating many Americans, who now often seem to be psychologically driven to get the latest hot products and do all the trendy new things.[93-94] This often resembles some Pavlovian nightmare, where hordes of drooling morons seem to be obsessed with purchasing anything American advertisers ordain. Things they often don't need and cannot afford. And thanks to modern technology, there is now no end to what one can buy. Examine any home and you will find attics, basements, closets and garages packed full of previous hot items. Many often go unused and are frequently resold at yard sales for a fraction of their original cost.

Needless shopping, just to survey new products, is now a very popular social activity. The resultant impulse buying is a big factor in the credit card debts of many U.S. families.[95-96] A person's convenience or revolving use of credit is seen to define their intelligence, social status and personal character. New regulations have raised credit card costs and made it much more difficult to declare bankruptcy. The pace of all this activity is constantly increasing so that ever more money can be grabbed by ever more unscrupulous profiteers. This often appears to be more of a predatory exploitation of mass psychology, than any sort of legitimate business enterprise. Many Americans have gotten to be so acclimated to living at a frantic pace that they find it very hard to ever slow down. And, thanks to cellular telephones, many Americans need never be alone again and they may never have to learn how to think for themselves.

America saw an explosion in materialism after World War II that has seemingly undermined any philosophical thought by its population. A big divide now separates European and American youth on many issues. While Europeans still seem to take some pride in appreciating higher education and the fine arts, many Americans are increasingly noted for their morbid obesity and ignorance of global concerns. American life seems to be driven by an obsessive satisfaction of personal comforts, hormones and vanity. The old American philosophy of Manifest Destiny has sown the seed of its demise by yielding a populace that cannot resist their most frivolous desires. This has now escalated to where America is rapidly devouring the whole world's natural resources, ruining its environment, destabilizing its economy and earning the contempt of thinking people everywhere. The word empathy, meaning sympathetic understanding, has even been removed from many new American dictionaries, because of its general lack of use.

Many foreign countries are still mad about the Millennial computer crisis. It is widely seen as a criminal American shakedown that needlessly cost the world $1.6-trillion ($10^{12}$).[97] No one can believe that the Americans could really be so stupid that they never anticipated the arrival of the year 2000. Of course, the profiteering designers of such con games are now busy dreaming up the next big extortion scheme. Their rapacious personalities seem to make them incapable of seeing any bigger picture at all, even as it literally destroys their own families.

Corporations now employ devious warranties and employment contracts which undermine consumer and employee legal rights by obligating them to settling any disputes by potentially biased arbitration. Corporate thefts from retirement funds cost U.S. workers some $450-billion, destroying many programs and leaving them with one-third of what they had been promised.[98]

Rich Americans are now being urged to set up lucrative tax shelters, disguised as charities, that aren't really charitable at all. Increasingly noted for their stinginess and insatiable greed, many CEOs now demand compensation packages over 200-times their average employee, damning some workers to a degrading poverty as cruelly as any Medieval tyrant.[99-102] Amoral investors seem to shut their eyes to all of the foul deeds that are done in their behalf. Is it unreasonable to restrain greed? Isn't that what the progressive income tax was meant to do? Today's productivity gains often seem to be dependent upon questionable accounting practices and the mandatory overtime work of employees. Many CEO's seem to prefer to exploit low-wage and illegal immigrants, or outsource work to low-wage countries, rather than hire the added employees that are needed to create better working conditions. Some impose such irresponsible toilet access restrictions, that they literally force some of their employees to wear disposable diapers.[103]

The average American now spends so much time working and commuting that they don't really have any meaningful family life. Statistics show they only have 2 to 3 minutes of daily conversation with their own children.[104] American infant mortality exceeds that in some underdeveloped countries. Meanwhile, the nation is literally awash in alcohol, drugs and guns.[105-107] Ritalin, a drug that is widely used for treating Attention Deficit and Hyperactivity Disorders, is prescribed 5-times more often in America than in Europe. One-fifth of America's children now exhibit signs of mental illness.[108-109] Wealthy Americans are secretly committing thousands of their own troubled children to scary behavior modification schools. Schools that are widely being seen as private prisons, costing up to $35,000 a year.[110]

America's children are often killing their parents and launching rampage killings at impersonal jumbo schools, designed primarily to enrich local real estate developers. Over 300 American parents are now being murdered annually by their own children. Disturbed adults are also committing unspeakable acts of child and spousal abuse, road rage and rampage killings of many sorts. The behavior of many children is seen to reflect their parent's frustrations. Over half of U.S. marriages now end in divorce, and 40 percent of its children are being born out of wedlock.[111] Ten children are killed every day by handguns, and half of all child sex abuse is now being committed by other children. Unsupervised children are now engaging in dangerous activities that are rooted in their ready access to their parent's alcohol, drugs, guns and pornography. While some 2-million Americans are hurt annually in serious crimes, 80 percent now go unsolved.

Despite America's grand display of religious faith, it often seems that those who proclaim their morality the loudest often tend to have the least.[112] Such ploys often seem to be designed to divert attention from an exploitive hidden agenda that involves swindling public programs, abusing some sector of the population, perpetuating needless wars, manipulating the stock market, or simply raping the environment. The U.S. psychological warfare training that's given exclusively to its military officers, often seems to end up being maliciously employed against unsuspecting fellow Americans, for political power or profit, when they then leave the service.[113] Aggressive military interrogation tactics have influenced civilian police procedures to where they are now noted for forcing false confessions from innocent people.[114-115]

Serving vast global industrial empires, the typical American CEO has now devotedly made its work force ever more mobile. Today, the average American now moves every three years. This has undermined many communities as well as families. Schools, churches and civic groups have suffered major losses of essential volunteers. Their own fleeting residence and oppressive work schedules means that many professionals invest very little effort in any community service. Moreover, their domineering and deceitful personalities often make them more of a liability than an asset. Dangerous confrontations have often occurred at many innocent social activities. Their golden parachute compensation packages then seem to guarantee that few of them ever really consider all of the local social or environmental consequences of their own corporate decisions.[99-102] And, while wealthy Americans frequently criticize the behavior of the local poor children, they blithely demand that their parents work long hours for unlivably low wages. International studies are now showing that it is far more difficult for the average person to get ahead in America today than it is in many of the world's more progressive nations.[116-120]

Americans often naively believe that advancing technology will magically solve almost any problem, without them doing anything at all. Yet, as the home of Hollywood, it should not be surprising that personal illusions are often deemed to be far more important than reality. Many are persuaded to ignore the fact that any solutions proposed might have hidden costs which could affect their family budget, lifestyle, environment and personal aspirations. Just like corporations, many have become highly acclimated to thinking in short monthly or quarterly accounting periods, rather than the far longer times that are often needed to shape any philosophic perspective. This then often makes them their own worst enemy.

Many even expect fusion energy to magically eliminate any need for energy conservation, and often embrace deceitful propaganda from corrupt profiteering organizations. This has often shut down many more sensible alternatives and encouraged an aggressive consumption of many nonrenewable or polluting resources.[79-81] Some nonsensical ideas seem to be only diversionary tactics that are designed to undermine sound energy conservation while perpetuating the existing economic status quo and the ongoing destruction of the environment.

Traditional energy suppliers often promoted risky expansions of domestic coal, oil and gas production. People were then encouraged to ignore the fact that such resources will be consumed with a nice profit for producers, while a consumer's own energy conservation can repeatedly save them real money year-after-year. Such thinking undermined the U.S. nuclear industry, which rushed ahead with building reactors without any plan for disposing of the radioactive waste. Disasters at Three Mile Island and Chernoble then destroyed the public support for nuclear power. America now has vast amounts of deadly radioactive waste and no good place to put it.[121-122] Its use of coal fired electric generators has also generated enormous amounts of CO_2 production, along with vast unstable impoundments of toxic coal ash.[123] Chris Mooney's book, *The Republican War on Science,* explores some of these American dilemmas.[124]

All of these aspects of modern civilization raise important questions which can't be excused by any political or religious rationalizations.[125] Moreover, if our actions and inactions clearly demonstrate that we are naturally self-destructive, it then makes our every pretense of integrity and intelligence a farce. This would threaten to reduce humanity itself to being little more than a vain, insidious, planetary disease. We should really then need to assess whether these obsessive compulsive tendencies aren't truly suicidal?

THE LEADERSHIP CHALLENGE

An old engineering analogy compares human nature to the working fluid in any hydraulic system. When you apply pressure, it always takes the easy way out. We all know that it's true. Rich or poor, educated or ignorant, young or old, when faced with any problem, our first instinct is to minimize doing anything at all. When it then becomes unavoidable, we still often tend to do only as little as necessary. Now, when the very survival of mankind is at stake, many fear that we have waited far too long.

Modern trade, travel and communication have turned our world into what Marshall McLuhan called a global village.[126] The speed with which it occurred has challenged our ability to cope with its effects.[127] Professional people are now hard pressed to even keep up with the developments in their specialty. Leaders must deal with problems that bewilder the smartest intellectuals. Those old consensus building techniques now seem inadequate. Groups have trouble staffing themselves to meet all the new requirements. Intrusive news media discourage potential candidates from seeking public office. Many offices are held by assertive people who only know how to seize power. Their tenure is then often undermined by an inability to build the cooperation that the job itself requires. Everyone is now being frustrated by the accelerating flood of information, obligations, threats

33

and diversions. Psychological denial is inhibiting us all from facing up to the fact that we are now a part of the problem. Time is running out for us to act, before the looming environmental and social crises undermine our lives. If we let this opportunity to pass, humanity will fail this fundamental test of its integrity and intelligence.[128-129]

The varied perceptions of time itself play a big role in the world at large. The geologist M. King Hubbert described our use of fossil fuels as a mere blip of geologic time.[130] He exposed the dilemma of utilizing any non-renewable resources, given our growing world population. As their popularity grows, their accelerating consumption then guarantees their rapid depletion. While America's latest oil discoveries seem large, they represent a limited supply at best. Too many people conveniently ignore the increased difficulty, danger and cost of tapping the new deposits. Conventional American oil production had peaked in 1970, as did the world output around 2005.[131] The full environmental and economic impact of tapping shale oil and tar sands deposits has yet to be assessed.

Although the pace of life will naturally vary with the geographic region and culture, technological change is literally affecting everyone, everywhere. Underdeveloped countries could well find their wealth of natural resources wasted by others, before they even recognized their real value. Many could end up with only the spoils of their good fortune, and be reduced to begging for help from the very robbers who came to call. Any generocity of the industrial nations may then be undercut by their own inability to perpetuate their former lifestyle. Their victims could then find themselves being exploited as toxic dumping grounds for foreign industrial waste.[132] Isolated by two big oceans, America had long been able to ignore the plight of the countries that it depended upon. Our evolving global village is now forcing everyone to reconsider those international relationships.[133]

Their philosophy and religion shape how any culture faces major problems.[134-137] And respectful discussion cannot be avoided for fear of offending anyone. Progress will then demand a fair and forthright confrontation of many such concerns. While philosophy explores human ethics and interaction, religion examines life's uncertainties related to our morality and mortality. Faced with a dangerous and bewildering world, many have sought psychological refuge in religious fundamentalism.[138] But, while religion may offer salvation and forgiveness of one's sins, it often ignores irresponsible behavior. Diverse views on sin and grace are clashing in very disconcerting ways. Too many seem to rationalize their personal sins as being automatically forgiven, due to their special relation with an Almighty God.[139]

Christian fundamentalists often appear ignorant of the Bible's political editing initiated by the Roman

Emperor Constantine.[140-145] But, believers of any sacred texts rarely understand their evolution. Corrupt aristocracies then aggressively encouraged ignorant peasants to seek their personal satisfaction in the afterlife, rather than challenge the status quo. Fundamentalists naturally like to dogmatically ordain the truth of the world, rather than deal objectively with anything. Damning any objective thinking for being politically correct, they long to impose their beliefs on others. Embittered by any rejection, some seek retribution against their detractors. The Jewish Torah, Christian New Testament and Moslem Koran all command their followers to punish unbelievers.[146-148] This can create animosity, much like the Holy Inquisition did back in Medieval Europe. America's own Alcoholic Prohibition crusade caused a major expansion of organized crime. Somehow, our new global village must now peacefully accommodate all of this accumulating diversity.

In 1844, a million American Millerites gave away their belongings to await Christ's triumphal return.[148] Now, Christian fundamentalists seem to endorse Israel's malicious treatment of Palestinians, while they still believe that Christ's triumphal return is imminent. A time when 'everyone' must embrace their beliefs or face utter damnation.[149-151] Yet, it is doubtful that any modern converts would be trusted any more than they have been in the past.[152] Many seem so frustrated with God's repeated failures to deliver the End Times, they think they might initiate it with violent confrontations.[153-154] They condemn any ecumenism and dream of shaping a new world to suit themselves. How do you best deal with such religious dogmatism? Christian evangelicals pretend to speak for all America, yet only one-in-four Christians and just one-in-seven Jews now attend regular services. And fundamentalists clearly produce their share of dysfunctional families and criminal activity.[155] Both political and religious leaders use diversionary tactics, phony dogma and apocalyptic threats to obstruct an objective resolution of any issues. Infanticide, abortion and artificial birth control were all known in the time of Jesus, who did not appear to preach against them.[140-141] Then too, denunciators often seem to be diverting attention from their own profiteering.[156]

Modern leaders must respectfully consider the world's diverse cultural history. In tribal areas, the family status, tradition and taboos clearly rule. Aristocracies then demand a need to know one's proper place and a concept of privilege for the chosen few. The colonial American idea of Manifest Destiny was a simple derivative of the old feudal aristocracy. It offered devotees the opportunity to become princes in realms of their own design. They only needed the will to aggressively exploit the people, resources and environment around them.[40] This yielded Machiavellian leaders who now see the whole world as ripe for their aggressive exploitation. An

37

ignorant and naive general public was then often physically and psychologically abused in a new sort of corporate serfdom. Playing a key role in America for 500 years, it is why its laws are notoriously deceitful, with loopholes to appease powerful interests, and why it now literally has half of the world's lawyers.[157] While the city of Paris may now have 3-times as many gourmet chefs as lawyers, that ratio is reversed in America. Manifest Destiny is behind the beliefs that bigger is always better and a use of creative accounting and subcontracting practices that dissipate accountability and clearly amplify the opportunities for corruption. Incapable of dealing with their personal failings, many such leaders then simply dismiss any criticism as mere jealousy. Anti-disparagement laws even suppress public criticism of entire industries.[158-159] This vain and selfish philosophy drives American political criticism of any concept of responsible world government and any objective rules of ethical behavior. Many Americans are now convinced that what really matters in life is what you can get away with, and not what is right or wrong. A nationwide poll by the magazine *U.S. News & World Report* showed that fully 84 percent of American college students believe that they need to cheat in order to get ahead.[160-162]

While formerly exploiting African slaves and Native Americans, modern Manifest Destiny devotees see the whole world offering major opportunities for their personal exploitation.[163] Edwin Black saw the International Business Machine Company having few qualms about helping Nazi Germany obtain equipment for the Holocaust.[164] America is now the world's largest arms dealer, selling 2.4-times the Russians, 5-times the French, and 15-times the Chinese.[165] Moreover, no other country has made more deadly weapons and training available to potential terrorists.[166]

The spirit of Manifest Destiny reverberated in America's 1980's Savings and Loan scandal that cost its taxpayers some $400-billion.[167] Its modern credit card companies then pushed families into huge debts, with annual interest rates up to 35 percent.[168] Predatory debt collectors helped to create spikes in U.S. bankruptcies, home foreclosures and suicides. It is also behind the push to get everyone into the stock market, where small investors finance its expansion, while insiders get really big payoffs. Enron, Worldcom and other corporate failures have documented the government's role in swindling its own citizens.[169] Acts that many have come to see as National Economic Treason.

Manifest Destiny is behind the U.S. popularity of poker with its bluff, bullying and bravado as opposed to the intellect, order and decorum of chess. Indeed, the Cold War can be seen as a sort of geopolitical chess game, where the USSR was seen as a master player. The Reagan administration then saw it as being more like poker, where capitalism's special economic flexibility allowed it to dramatically raise the stakes, via defense spending, to where the USSR could simply no longer compete. Reagan supporters really believed that Russia never had a chance, even though they undermined the American economy by literally tripling the national debt.[170]

Despite America's grandiose pretense of morality, Manifest Destiny makes dealing with its prior victims difficult. Devotees fear such efforts could get out of hand, restricting access to the next big opportunity. Exceptions emerged where some learned how to play the game for themselves. Some Native Americans exploited legalities allowing them to open new casinos. Reparations have even been made to the Japanese Americans who were incarcerated in World War II. And Nelson Rockefeller had provided key support for establishing the state of Israel, after they threatened to expose his business relations with Nazi Germany.[171] Israel's creation then involved the forced expulsion of Arabs and absorbing millions of European Jews, that America didn't want.[172-173] The United States then provided all of the aid needed for Israel to flourish, while it abused the Palestinians much like the U.S. had treated its own Native Americans. It even opted to ignore Israel's attempt to sink the USS Liberty.[174]

Albert Einstein criticized Israel's creation as a fascist development and declined their invitation to be its first head of state.[175] Many now see Israel as a covert

American Protectorate, whose economic prosperity and military adventures depend upon its annual funding, Table 3.[176] Aid to Egypt began in 1978 under Jimmy Carter, as an incentive to make peace with Israel. That assistance was slashed by President Obama. America's minor foreign aid budget exposes it as one of the stingiest industrial nations. While other nations generally gave cold hard cash equal to over one percent of their gross domestic product, America gave only 0.15 percent. And that usually consisted of special vouchers, good only for buying its surplus agriculture and military production.[177]

Table 3: Major 1999 U.S. Foreign Aid Recipients

	Aid (millions)	Population (millions)	Aid per Capita
Israel*	$2,940	5.75	$511.30
Egypt	$2,161	67.27	$32.12
Russia	$689	146.39	$4.71
Jordan	$290	4.56	$63.58
Ukraine	$228	49.81	$4.58
Colombia	$212	39.31	$5.39
Indonesia	$205	216.11	$0.95

* In 2003 Israel sought to have its annual aid increased to $15-billion.

Unscrupulous people everywhere have learned from America's demonstrations of Manifest Destiny. Ending the Cold War has left just one superpower and many fear such power will invariably be abused.[178-179] The Cold War cost its taxpayers several trillion dollars, yet it is now known to been based on exaggerated threats that never existed.[180] This deceit had eniched phony

41

industrial patriots and profiteers, who extorted enormous power and profits from the paranoia that they had wantonly created. The U.S. defense budget was $768-billion in 2021. This exceeds the rest of the world combined and did not include any war expenditures.[181] One-tenth goes to Black Operations that are considered to be exempt from all national and international laws.[182]

These rogue activities defile any claim that America is a respectable democracy. They notoriously provide plausible deniability to the presidents who initiate them and produced legions of direct and collateral victims. And it is now feared that some military industrialists have covertly assumed a similar sort of authority.[183] Seen as inherently deceitful, U.S. foreign policy often demonstrates a paranoid fear that everyone else is surely just as bad.[184-187] America now leads the world in producing sociopathic type people. Indeed, the famed Milgram studies showed that most Americans were clearly vulnerable to obeying malevolent authority.

Many fear military extortion may be the only way to perpetuate America's wanton waste of world resources. U.S. neoconservatives lobby for ever more defense spending and seem eager to exploit the War-on-Terror as a profiteering Cold War substitute.[188] The University of Chicago's Leo Strauss and Milton Friedman had encouraged the aggressive use of propaganda to help obscure America's Machiavellian agenda.[189-191] This strategy secretly manipulated the public with its deceitful use of words like Christian, democracy, freedom, justice, liberty and patriot. While federal controls restricted industrial profits in World War II, those are all gone now. This dramatically increased the Pentagon's cost of doing anything and led to its systemic corruption.[192-193] Military industrial companies literally became addicted to this lucrative situation, with many infatuated with the enormous profits that were available from America's Black Budget operations. In the book *Crisis and Leviathan*, Robert Higgs noted: "That never did so many prosper so much by feeding on fear." [194]

Its Unacknowledged Special Access Projects had caused serious American anxiety about the formation of the new International Criminal Court.[195-196] It feared it might see prosecution for faking the 1964 Tonkin Gulf incident, used to expand the war in Vietnam.[197-198] A money making sort of conflict that had killed some 58-thousand Americans and 3.8-million Vietnamese. They also fear charges of waging chemical warfare in Vietnam, using some 21-million gallons of dioxin laced Agent Orange; the Phoenix Program, where American death squads tortured 67,000 civilian men, women and children, killing some 30 percent;[199] as well as Operation Speedy Express, that had launched monthly My Lai type massacres.[200] And fear prosecution for their biological assault on Cuba, using African Swine Fever to decimate its hog production, as well as contaminating large foreign areas with cluster munitions, toxic depleted

43

uranium projectiles, and anti-personnel mines.[201-202] Finally, it fears potential criminal charges for killing and overthrowing many key foreign leaders, who it replaced with compliant dictators like Saddam Hussein, Augusto Pinochet and the hated Shah of Iran.[195-196]

The 11 September 2001 terroist attacks were a wake-up call from America's accumulating enemies.[203] Killing over 2,700 people in New York's World Trade Center, they were condemned all around the world. However, many were surprised by George W. Bush's dismay that anyone could hate the United States. Yet, few Americans seem to appreciate the great anger that many U.S. actions have provoked abroad.[204] Although both America and Britain now suffer from the illegal drug trade, they are considered its creators. This is due to the 1839 Opium War, forcing China to accept opium as money. They were both also big operators in the hated slave trade, and behind many of the problems in Northern Ireland and Middle East.

All of humanity was debased by Adolf Hitler's final solution to his Jewish problem. Yet, an evil aspect of any abusive situation is that all too often the victims seem to be prone to becoming future abusers.[205-206] Who can really ignore the ugly parallels between U.S. treatment of Native Americans, Israel's of Palestinians and Hitler's abuse of the Jews? This includes Israel's racist legislation and its own launching of Middle East terrorism.[207] We might add their criminal occupation of refugee camps; forcing

44

Arab civilians to strip naked at gunpoint; incarcerating people without trial; their wide use of torture [shaping U.S. action in Iraq[208]]; blocking outside aid and observers from many situations; massive demolishion of Arab homes and infrastructure; committing numerous assassinations; and their using deadly American weapons to crush a clearly disarmed and desperate people, enraged to where their suicidal 'counterterrorism' was seen as their only recourse.[209] This nazi-like character of right-wing Israelis would seem to be Hitler's darkest legacy. Israel now spends 30 percent more for its defense than all of its Arab neighbors combined.[210-211] With its generous U.S. assistance, tiny Israel is now the world's fourth largest arms dealer. Its powerful political lobby threatens to destroy any American politician showing respect for Palestinian rights.[212-215] Israelis leaders are now calling American Jews who dare to criticize Israel, 'Self-Hating' Jews, provoking a new Exodus from Judaism.[216-217]

It is seemingly asserted that Hitler's extermination of the Jews was the historically definitive Holocaust.[218] Yet, how does anyone rank the horrors that humanity has now wantonly inflicted upon their fellow man? Was the Nazi killing of Jews worse than their killing of the Slavs or Roma? What about the European extermination of Native Americans, the American enslavement of Africans and its brutal colonization of the Philippines? And what about Australia's killing Aborigines, Belgium's raping the Congo, Turkey's slaughtering Armenians, the Papal genocide of the Cathars, Joseph Stalin's starving Ukrainians, Japan's raping Nanking, Croatia's extermination of the Serbs, Yugoslavia's killing Albanians, or the Jew's biblical genocide of the Canaanites? And the list just goes on and on. Clearly, no one is above reproach. Are justifiable self-defense and aggression now really only appropriate for the United States and Israel? History is full of aggressors who were seeking new land to accommodate their growing populations.[219-221]

The Soviet Union's collapse encouraged a closer examination of modern capitalism.[222] America now covertly suppresses free enterprise and cooperative ventures in serving huge multi-national corporations. Firms that are often accused of using their wealth and power to fix prices and corrupt local officials.[223-225] Some nations, devastated in World War II, had reaped democratic benefits from a reconstruction process that forced all segments of their society to then work together.[226] That social fairness was damned as being socialist, even communist, by Manifest Destiny zealots. Europe's open planning and compensation debates contrasted sharply with the situation existing in the United States.

America has literally waged psychological warfare against its own people. World War II casualties were listed as: (1) *Killed in Action*; (2) *Killed in Action-Body Not Recovered*; or (3) *Missing in Action*. The designation *Killed in Action-Body Not Recovered* was

46

reserved for situations that had been witnessed to be inescapable. President Nixon then prolonged the Vietnam War and dampened widespread public opposition by changing casualties listed 'Killed in Action-Body Not Recovered' to 'Missing in Action-Prisoner of War'.[227] This political tactic was further exploited by Ronald Reagan in order to divert public attention from his economic destruction of the American Savings and Loans.[167] He also spread unfounded rumors North Vietnam had not returned all of our POWs and that many were still languishing in tiger cages, just like we had held the Vietnamese.[197-198] Worried about loved ones, many American families were then targeted by crooks who deceitfully proposed to rescue their loved ones in Veitnam, Rambo style.[228]

Although America loudly expresses fears terrorists might conceivably use weapons of mass destruction, it is really their one and only primary user. It was so eager to obtain Japanese biological weapons research, after World War II, that it overlooked their actually having been tested on its U.S. and British POWs. America's arsenal was once overflowing with nuclear, biological and chemical weapons. Developments that are suspected of causing America's own plagues of Lyme disease, West Nile Virus and other ailments.[201] George W. Bush had repudiated prior deals with the USSR and declared that nuclear weapons, slated for disposal, would now only be retired. He put the world on notice that he would launch a massive nuclear response to any perceived or imagined threats.[229-230] While forcing other nations to then sign a Nuclear Non-Proliferation Treaty, he permitted Israel's assertive development, production and deployment of nuclear weapons.[231] In 1973, Israel threatened to use them if America did not immediately resupply its conventional weapons for the looming Yom Kippur war with Egypt. Israel now possesses hundreds of low yield nuclear missiles, artillery shells, land mines and suitcase bombs.

America's two-party politics has degenerated to where each side constantly tears down the other's work to replace it with their own, undermining any enduring national progress.[232-234] Its believers in democracy have gravitated into the Democratic Party, while Manifest Destiny zealots are today's Republicans. While Democrats clearly support welfare for the poor, Republicans want it done away with and replaced by corporate plenty for the rich.[235] Many social welfare laws go unenforced, while legislation is loaded with earmarks rewarding exploitive lobbyists, who now actually write much of America's legislation.[236-239] While the Democrats encourage everyone to vote, Republicans want it to be restricted to their own supporters.[240-241] American elections are now dominated by huge costs and special interest contributors. Many now fear that any election reforms will be easily circumvented.[242-244] Only one-third of potential voters, one-sixth under thirty, register and vote in elections that many call farcical.[245]   Erich Fromm warned us that many would be naturally intimidated by the responsibility of democracy and they would psychologically escape by leaving it to others.[246]

America is now mired in a subtle sort of civil war that churns its economy in ways that impoverish the general population while enriching its aristocracy.[247-248] The drive to privatize Social Security is just one such Republican Party maneuver. While the Republicans use anti-monopoly laws to undermine labor rights, they ignore wrongdoing by corporate conglomerates. It is feared that America is now a covert corporate fascist dictatorship, where its sociopathic CEOs are literally being empowered to ravage the planet.[222] Corporate media takeovers seem to foster a biased, cowardly, dumbed down and low cost journalism.[249-252]

Many people questioned George W. Bush's and Donald Trump's generous tax relief for the wealthy, big defense budgets, trade deficits and national debts.[253] Repairing America's crumbling infrastructure yields twice as many jobs as any money spent on defense, but war is the ultimate money maker in the USA. While its leaders have demanded full transparency and accountability from others, they seem truly devious. Allies have called us a bully who tells others what to do, while it refuses to put its own house in order.[254-258]   We are seen as recklessly painting others as evil boogeymen, just to divert attention from ourselves. U.S. healthcare is the worst in the industrial world, costing twice as much per citizen as effective foreign programs.[259-260] People of color routinely experience substandard education, poor healthcare, police brutality, impoverishment and voter disenfranchisement.[261-263]

The world dreads that America, or its surrogate Israel, could launch military action anytime its strategic resources are at stake and its defense industry offers politicians an attractive kill ratio.[264-265] Both Christian Dominionists and Republican Neocons seem to think the most heinous acts become righteous when they are committed for God.[155] America's great citizen soldiers of World War II, representing all segments of society, are long gone.[266] Eliminating the draft appears to have put American war profiteers in charge of foreign affairs. Abusive redeployments, stop-loss service extensions and call-ups of long dismissed personnel are common. High unemployment pushed many into the military.[267-269] Local recruiters are now accused of lying to gullible teenagers and accepting convicted criminals to meet their high quotas. Many are promised signing bonuses, special training or base assignments, even freedom from combat, that often disappear when they report for duty. U.S. military crime, divorce, suicide, drug abuse and psychiatric problems have skyrocketed. One thousand patients a month attempt suicide at its military hospitals.

One-in-three women in the military are now being sexually assaulted.[270-271] The U.S. Air Force Academy seems to subject students to assertive evangelical proselytizing, while it seemingly condones the raping of female cadets.[272-273] As a whole, the women in America are 8-times more likely to be raped as those in Italy.[274] This yields about 25,000 babies annually, with many sold on the black market by Christian rape profiteers. The U.S. trivialization of rape dates back to when Black and Native American women were wantonly abused by white settlers.[275] Now, prostitutes serving U.S. military personnel are spreading a dangerous new, drug resistant, strain of gonorhea.[276]

Nothing has undermined U.S. integrity more than its covert operations, which many believe are out of control.[277] These crimes against U.S. and international law consume one tenth of its defense budget, which exceeds the entire defense budgets of many other countries.[182,203] Modern weapons now permit American presidents to unleash their wrath with a truly godlike rage. Some even suspect that the CIA murdered Sweden's prime minister, Olof Palme, in 1986.[278] Unaffected by ending the Cold War, its Black Operations have earned global contempt and provoked many terrorist acts.[203] The CIA's own Guerrilla Warfare Manual is now the primary textbook utilized in terrorist training camps around the world.

While some American Black Ops have been funded off-the-books by foreign governments, others have supposedly used profits from illegal drug sales or World War II Axis loot.[279] Its failure to account for this recovered treasure, or provide any fair return to its original owners, reflects its Manifest Destiny morality. This would even seem to make all of its leaders, from Harry Truman to Joe Biden, accessories in Axis atrocities. The 1951 secret Treaty of San Francisco, relinquishing Japanese war reparations, was believed to mask an agreement to literally split the loot. It supposedly forbade compensation for any of the U.S. and British POWs who were tortured in Japanese germ warfare experiments, or buried alive with its hidden plunder.

Black Operations impose a compartmented, need to know, secrecy that is contemptuous of democracy. Information needed for vital democratic decisions is now hidden from politicians and citizens alike.[280-282] Plagued with untold casualties, those involved are threatened with heavy fines and imprisonment for disclosing any classified information.[283] Many are believed murdered or medically shut-up to protect presidential plausible deniability.[284-285] Psychosurgery, using computer controlled beams of gamma radiation, can now create brain lesions mimicking Alzheimer's disease.[286] Wild conspiracy theories have been promoted to hide the truth amongst all of the resulting confusion.[195] Many CIA operations involved spying and psywar action against Americans. Although Frank Church's 1975 Senate Committee condemned the agencies involved, those responsible clearly went unpunished. NSA electronic surveillance, developed with the UK, now allows America to eavesdrop on Britains for Britain, while they spy on

Americans for America, circumventing the existing laws in both nations.[287]   Bush set up secret torture facilities around the world, violating local sovereignty and the Geneva Conventions.[288] This Extraordinary Rendition represented the contract torture of some American prisoners by other countries.   An illegal practice that was launched by Bill Clinton.

Senator Frank Church tried to stop the notorious Operation MK-ULTRA electromagnetic mind control experiments.   These had exposed American soldiers to mood altering radiation on Long Island, New York in the 1950s.[289-291]   They documented our vulnerability to low frequency pulses of radio frequencies, like 425 megahertz, that resonate inside of our brain.[292-296] The Soviet Lida Machine was said to use this effect to make American POWs confess to Korean war crimes. Low power pulses, at 8 to 12 hertz, are believed to stimulate an alpha brain state that then opens the subconscious mind to accept almost any proposition. Some subjects were supposedly made to compulsively express bizarre beliefs, like being stationed on Mars, that were designed to destroy their credibility.   This research reflected the Pentagon's reckless use of microwave technology, commonly exposing American personnel to 1,000-times the radiation level that was seen in Russia.[293-298]

The 2001 PATRIOT Act exploited the anger over the 9/11 attacks.   Drafted well before 9/11, they were rapidly approved without any study or debate.[299-302]

This gave G. W. Bush the right to secretly arrest, try and dispose of anyone, including U.S. citizens, that he deemed Unlawful Enemy Combatants. He described this 342-page tome as simply clarifying existing law. The 2006 Military Commissions Act then actually terminated American's right of Habeas Corpus to fight unwarranted arrest, and the 2007 John Warner Act dramatically simplified the use of U.S. troops against fellow Americans.[303-313] George W. Bush then often added Signing Statements to legislation to restrict its execution, and labeled documents 'Pre-Decisional' to exempt them from the Freedom of Information Act. He also suppressed data on the huge numbers of Iraqi civilians that were killed, maimed, imprisoned, or made destitute by the U.S.[314-322] He even promoted unfounded fears of Iranian and Iraqi nuclear weapons at a time when some 4,300 kilograms of fissile, bomb grade, material was actually lost in America.[323]

Republican Neocons and Christian Dominionists were seen as America's 'Manifest Destiny' zealots.[155] They represented capitalism run amok, devoid of social constraints that Adam Smith deemed essential.[324-329] George W. Bush had pandered to the vanity, fears and ignorance of many Americans to win election.[242] Dr. Bryant Welch offered a psychological analysis of Bush's campaign in the book *State of Confusion*.[330] The endemic new Republican philosophy of taking abusive and undue advantage of fellow Americans has now undermined empathy in America, turning it into a playground for liars, bullies, crooks and lawyers.[331-333] Bush had obediently served the interests of energy, defense and financial companies. This had included the Bush Family Dynasty, said to be based upon his grandfather's loyal financial service to Nazi Germany.[334] The Koch brothers, using a fortune that was derived from their father's industrial service to Joseph Stalin, launched the notorious Republican Tea Party.[335-339]

Few Americans realize pricing world commodities in dollars subsidizes their lifestyles at foreign expense. Two-thirds of U.S. currency is located abroad and America controls both the International Monetary Fund and World Bank.[163] G. W. Bush had stopped publishing data on America's money supply, fueling speculation that he was secretly printing money for some hidden agenda.[340]   U.S. presidents often behave like Wall Street puppets.   The 2008 recession involved phony investments, called Collateralized Debt Obligations. These were financial derivatives based on subprime real estate mortgages.[341-364]   The seemingly growing corruption of America's legislative, executive and judicial processes, via lobbying and revolving-door employment, now seems malignant.[365-381]   The Pentagon was even found unable to account for $8.5-trillion in spending.[239] Yet, neither political party really appears to grasp the impending peril of this evolving political dilemma.[335]

Today, many Americans are simply ignorant of the real wars that are right now erupting all around them. As problem solvers, engineers learn that the first step in properly correcting any problem is to expose its existence to everyone whose personal assistance may then be needed to solve it. However, this becomes a real challenge when the problem involves all of our natural human frailties. It does not take a genius to know that the greatest potential of any nation lies in getting all of its people pulling together, instead of pulling apart. American democracy was a bold historic experiment that depended upon continually educating every one of its citizen on the vital importance of building practical cooperation in an increasingly diverse society. With advancing technology shrinking our world into a global village, all of us are now far more dependent upon each other than many Americans seem to appreciate.

While it can be said that the vengeful conclusion of World War I had set the stage for Adolf Hitler and World War II, the vengeful conclusion of the Cold War then clearly set the stage for Vladimir Putin, Donald Trump and a new hybrid World War III. Few know of the secret operations and dogmatic forces that are now driving our modern reality. As the USSR collapsed, the CIA had supposedly launched a secret assault on its economy, in collaboration with the modern Russian Mafia, to destroy any chance of the USSR being reconstituted. Then, out of the subsequent economic devastation, Russian pride reasserted itself in the leadership of a former KGB bureaucrat named Vladimir Putin.

Bitter over getting kicked when they were down, he launched a fantastical quest to renew Russia's glorious past via a new type of hybrid warfare. A cause that was then spurred on by the economic sanctions imposed for his seizure of the Crimean Peninsula in 2014.

Hybrid warfare employs all of the cyber, psychological and disinformation arts developed during the Cold War. Activities that have been made all the more insidious and powerful by modern electronics, the Internet and social media. Putin aims to undermine world democracy everywhere, doing special harm to the United States. General Valery Gerasimov developed their new tactical concept of hybrid war to destroy America. It seeks to destroy us from within, keeping us all in the dark as to our own personal role in literally destroying our own nation. This involves close coordination of disinformation, cyber, electronic, and psychological tactics in order to overwhelm the nation and the social cohesiveness needed to hold it all together. If you can undermine that, then violent social chaos and national disintegration are sure to follow. Putin knows that our personal ignorance, fears and bigotries are any nation's vulnerable Achilles heel. With Donald Trump's inside assistance, wittingly or unwittingly, the Russians then sought to motivate all of our worst instincts. Whether it involves undermining the integrity of our elections, swamping our borders with hordes of Latin American refugees, or stirring up new terroristic concerns, their common objective is to destroy every American's confidence in their own country.

Will his battalions of Russian cyber soldiers use the Internet to mess up the delivery of your Social Security checks, or shut down your local water, gas, electric, cellphone, or transportation services? What about the operation of your bank, factory, hospital, or school? Will they use social media to spread hateful rumors about you, your family, race, religion, or group that then have your neighbors all up in arms after YOU? Will they even convince you that COVID vaccination and global warming are just hoaxes, so that you do nothing until it is simply too late? Will they use HAARP high power radio transmitters to bounce modulated signals off of the ionosphere to yield great blasts of trumpets in the sky, convincing eager religious believers that it's the Second Coming? What kind of scary psychological hoops might General Gerasimov have you then jumping through, like some frantic circus clown? In no time at all, our new hybrid war could literally have everyone out to murder one another, for no good reason at all.

Vladimir Putin's senseless 2022 invasion of Ukraine was a vain effort to restore Russia's historic greatness. However, time marches onward and only fools ever think that they might, somehow, turn back the clock. No amount of wishful thinking or Russian firepower would seem to be able to compell today's free-thinking citizens of Ukraine to bow down before Putin's fantasies. Russia's willfully ignorant population, deprived of free speech and the constant victims of state propaganda, appeared to swallow Putin's every lie and delusion. Now, in his resorting to a massive military campaign of wanton death and destruction, Russia's Vladimir Putin has become a truly Hitleric war criminal. His creation of millions of Ukrainian refugees has helped to galvanize the whole world against him. And thanks to modern technology, his every exploit is being documented on world television in a fashion that threatens to make him one of the world's most hated historic monsters. People everywhere are witnessing his atrocities in a way that has consolidated formal world condemnation. Comprehensive economic sanctions against Russia and the extensive Ukrainian military support, from Russia's surrounding NATO countries, could well be insurmountable, given the courage of the Ukrainians. And all of this is now happening in spite of Russia's suicidal capacity to wreak global nuclear anihilation. Yet, one has to wonder, if but for the CIA's suspected covert ruble ripoff operation, might Russian leadership have taken a much different path after the Cold War?

CONCLUSION

America would now appear to be the victim of a malignant psychological disorder that has amplified and entrenched its insanely arrogant hypocrisy.[382-384] Nowadays, people all over the world wonder if any justice can exist if America's leaders are seemingly deemed to be exempt from all law? No national constitution can really mean anything if it is not clearly understood and assertively enforced. Surely, Americans must be held accountable to the same standards that they would impose on others. Moreover, the world must beware of anyone promoting any unfounded fear and chaos. All leaders need to sever any ties with profiteering special interests if they are to seriously champion any responsible international meritocracy. America's super capitalists do not really represent free enterprise because they want all of the rules tailored to serve their own vulgar megalomania. Manifest Destiny ordains that its mega corporations have all the rights of individual citizens, when they are actually greed driven entities demanding serious regulation.[385-389] America must formally renounce its Manifest Destiny philosophy, Black Budget and imperial occupations of places like Okinawa and Quantanamo.[390-396] Instant Runoff voting procedures could potentially help to moderate its two-party politics.[397] And the simple ability to vote for 'None-of-the-Above' would give everyone the chance to put any problem politicians 'On Notice'.

Thomas Jefferson saw Constitutional Conventions occurring regularly to clarify, update and improve any government. This then offered to renew the national commitment to its vital support and enforcement. Scheduled for 1976, it was abruptly cancelled by an American legislature that was then corrupted by power. Had it taken place back in those more amenable times, it may have helped us to avoid the seeming hellscape that is now on our horizon. Hopefully, this process might be greatly facilitated by our modern Internet. A new Constitutional Convention would provide an very important opportunity to redefine the roles and responsibilities of the government and citizens alike. This must surely include rigorous new standards for reporting national economic, environmental and social statistics as well as public audits of the U.S. Treasury and Federal Reserve. It must offer global leadership by example, not intimidation. The United Nations itself should be reshaped into a confederation of 'only' those nations that are truly committed to a new constitution that deals effectively with today's needs.[398] This must comprehensively unite everyone around the world with a new type of Global Social Contract allowing everyone to hold each other accountable.[399-400] The U.N. General Assemby needs to formally vote on a constitutional amendment demanding the immediate and unequivocal revoking of partisan veto capabilities, so that it can now truly become the egalitarian world governing institution that it was originally meant to be.

Thomas E. Loxley

BIBLIOGRAPHY

1. DOUBER, P. M. & R. A. MULLER *The Three Big Bangs*, Addison Wesley, New York 1996.
2. ROSENBERG, M. *Current World Population and World Population Growth Since the Year One* at www.geography,about.com.
3. Article: *Population 7 Billion* by Robert Hunzig in <u>National Geographic</u>, p. 42-66, Jan 2011.
4. HECHT, J. *Vanishing Life*, Charles Scribner's Sons, New York 1993.
5. ERICKSON, J. *The Living Earth*, Facts On File, New York 2001.
6. KEYS, D. *Catastrophe*, Ballantine Books, New York 1999.
7. DARWIN, C. *The Origin of the Species*, A Mentor Book, New York 1958.
8. PEARCE, F. *The Coming Population Crash*, Beacon Press, Boston 2010.
9. KIERNAN, S. P. *Last Rights*, St. Martin's Press, New York 2006.
10. MARTENSEN, R. *A Life Worth Living*, Farrar, Straus & Giroux, New York 2008.
11. EHRLICH, P. R. & A. H. *The Population Explosion*, Simon & Schuster, New York 1990.
12. BROWN, L. R. *World Without Borders*, Vintage Books, New York 1972.
13. TAYLOR, G. R. *The Doomsday Book*, Fawcett Publications, Greenwich, CT 1970.
14. HEFFERNAN, M. *Willful Blindness*, Walker & Co, New York 2011.
15. *The World Almanac Book of Facts 2002*, World Almanac Books, New York.
16. LORENZ, K. *On Aggression*, Bantam Books, New York 1966.
17. EISELEY, L. *The Firmament of Time*, p. 133, Atheneum Publishers, New York 1960.
18. PERKINSON, R. *Texas Tough*, Metropolitan Books/Henry Holt & Co, New York 2010.
19. MAUER, M. *Race to Incarcerate*, The New Press, New York 2006.
20. Article: *Schizophrenic killer* by Mac McClelland in <u>Mother Jones</u>, p. 16-63, May/June 2013.
21. HOFSTADTER, R. *Anti-Intellectualism in American Life*, Alfred A. Knopf, New York 1963.
22. BERMAN, M. *Twilight of American Culture*, W. W. Norton & Co, New York 2001.
23. LEPRE, G. *Fragging*, Texas Tech U. Press, Lubbock, TX 2002.
24. Author served as elected local precinct election official in PA for 9 years.
25. PATTERSON, T. *The Vanishing Voter*, Alfred A. Knopf, New York 2002.
26. Article: *The magic mountain* by Matthew Power in <u>Harper's Magazine</u>, p. 57-68, Dec 2006.
27. NUSSBAUM, M. C. *The Clash Within*, Belknap Press of Harvard U., Cambridge, MA 2007.
28. WARD, P. M. *Colonias and Public Policy in Texas and Mexico*, U. Texas Press, Austin, TX 1999.
29. Article: *A special moment in history* by Bill McKibben in <u>Atlantic Monthly</u>, p. 55-78, May 1998.
30. COHEN, J. E. *How Many People Can the World Support?*, W.W. Norton & Co, New York 1995.
31. BROWN, L. *A Strategy to Stabilize World Population*, W.W. Norton & Co, New York 1974.
32. SCHNEIDER, S. H. *The Coevolution of Climate and Life*, Sierra Club, San Francisco 1984.

33. Article: *Refugee* at www.wikipedia.org.
34. BOURNE, R. *Gods of War - Gods of Peace*, Harcourt, New York 2002.
35. JACKSON, H. H. *A Century of Dishonor*, Ross & Haines, Minneapolis 1964.
36. ZINN, H. *A Peoples History of the U. S. 1492 - Present,* Harper Perennial, New York 1995.
37. *Eating Fire, Tasting Blood,* Marijo Moore ed, Thunder's Mouth Press, New York 2006.
38. JAHODA, G. *The Trail of Tears*, Wings Books, New York 1995.
39. *The Slavery Reader*, G. Heumon & J. Walvin eds., Routledge, Taylor & Francis, New York 2003.
40. WEINBERG, A. K. *Manifest Destiny*, Quadrangle Books, Chicago 1963.
41. HAYNES, S. R. *Noah's Curse*, Oxford U. Press, New York 2002.
42. LUNDBERG, F. *The Rich and the Super-Rich*, Bantam Books, New York 1968.
43. DOMHOFF, G. W. *The Higher Circles*, Random House, New York 1970.
44. PHILLIPS, P. M. *A Relative Advantage*, U. California, Davis 1994.
45. ROTHKOPF, D. *Super Class*, Farrar, Straus & Giroux, New York 2009.
46. HAWKEN, P. *The Ecology of Commerce*, Collins Business, New York 1993.
47. PIGOU, A. C. *The Economics of Welfare*, Macmillan & Co, London 1932.
48. FRIEDMAN, B. *The Moral Consequences of Economic Growth*, Vintage Books, New York 2003
49. *The Poisoned Well*, E. P. Jorgensen ed., Sierra Club/Island Press, Washington 1989.
50. PACKARD, V. *The Waste Makers*, Pocket Books, New York 1963.
51. BERRY, W. *The Unsettling of America*, Sierra Club Books, San Francisco 1977.
52. SCHUSKY, E. L. *Culture and Agriculture*, Bergin & Garver, Westport, CT 1989.
53. WILSON, E. O. *The Future of Life*, Alfred A. Knopf, New York 2002.
54. ELLIS, R. *The Empty Ocean*, Island Press/Shearwater Books, Washington 2003.
55. Article: *Ocean noise* by Leslie Allen in National Geographic, p. 28-31, Jan 2011.
56. BROWN, M. H. *Laying Waste*, Pantheon Books, New York 1979.
57. KIRBY, D. *Animal Factory*, St. Martin's Press, New York 2010.
58. HAUTER, W. *Foodopoly*, The New Press, New York 2012.
59. BROADHURST, C. L. *Diabetes: Prevention and Cure*, Kensington Books, New York 1999.
60. Article: *Intensive pig farming* on Internet at www.en.wikipedia.org.
61. Article: *Hell in high water* by D. Whitman in U. S. News & World Report, p. 22, 4 Oct 1999.
62. Article: *Gagged by big ag* by Ted Genoways in Mother Jones, p. 40-63, Jul/Aug 2013.
63. Article: *Colony collapse* by A. Kimble-Evans in Mother Earth News, Oct 2009.
64. Article: *Toxic inaction* by Mark Schapiro in Harper's Magazine, p. 78-83, Oct 2007.
65. RAPP, D. J. *Our Toxic World*, Environmental Research Foundation, Buffalo, NY 2004.
66. Article: *Criminal element* by Kevin Drum in Mother Jones, p. 28-62, Jan/Feb 2013.
67. Article: *Mountaintop mining consequences* by Margaret A. Palmer et al in Science Magazine, p. 148-149, 8 Jan 2010.
68. SHNAYERSON, M. *Coal River*, Farrar, Strauss & Giroux, New York 2008.

69. HUMES, E. *Garbology*, Avery/Penguin, New York 2012.
70. Article: *With a splash of VOCs* by A. Spake in U.S. News & World Report, p. 86, 6 Dec 1999.
71. Article: *MTBE ground water contamination*, U.S. News & World Report, p. 57, 3 Apr 2000.
72. Article: *The future of oil* by Bryan Walsh in TIME Magazine, p. 28-35, 9 Apr 2012.
73. KLARE, M. T. *The Race for What's Left*, Metropolitan Books/Henry Holt & Co, New York 2012.
74. JUHASZ, A. *Black Tide*, John Wiley & Sons, Hoboken 2011.
75. Article: *Fracking nation* by Linda Marsa in Discover Magazine, p. 62-70, May 2011.
76. Article: *Crude conundrum-Canada's tar sands* by J. Mark in Earth Island Journal, p. 34-42, Spring 2011.
77. Article: *Aging gas pipes at risk of explosion* by G. Burke & J. Dearan, Assoc Press,14 Sep 2000.
78. Article: *List of pipeline accidents* at www.wikipedia.org.
79. BLACK, E. *Internal Combustion*, St. Martin's Press, New York 2006.
80. JUHASZ, A. *The Tyranny of Oil*, Harper Collins, New York 2008
81. TAMMINEN, T. *Lives per Gallon*, Island Press/Shearwater Books, Washington 2009.
82. Article: *Why the U.S. may owe Indians untold billions* by D. Whitman in U.S. News & World Report, p. 24, 8 Mar 1999.
83. Article: *List of countries by energy consumption per capita* at www.wikipedia.org.
84. SCHOR, J. B. *The Overspent American*, Basic Books, New York 1998.
85. MARRS, J. *The Rise of the Fourth Reich*, William Morrow/Harper Collins, New York 2008.
86. PHILLIPS, K. *Bad Money*, Viking, New York 2008.
87. Article: *The real jobless rate* by Justin Fox in TIME Magazine, p. 39, 21 Dec 2009.
88. Article: *Too fast to fail* by Nick Baumann in Mother Jones, p. 36-41, Jan/Feb 2013.
89. deGraaf, J. et al *Affluenza: The All-Consuming Epidemic*, Berrett-Koehler, San Francisco 2001.
90. Article: *Plugging the kegs* by J. Thompson in U. S. News & World Report, p.63-67,26 Jan 1998.
91. ROSENBERG, T. *Join the Club*, W.W. Norton & Co, New York 2011.
92. Article: *The prison paradox* by E. Cose in Newsweek, p. 40-49, 13 Nov 2000.
93. JOHNSTON, D. C. *The Fine Print*, Portfolio/Penguin, New York 2012.
94. PACKARD, V. *The Hidden Persuaders*, Pocket Books, New York 1958.
95. WHYBROW, P. C. *American Mania*, W. W. Norton & Co, New York 2005.
96. PIERCE, C. P. *Idiot America*, Anchor, New York 2010.
97. Article: *Leadership for crisis resolution-the Y2K challenge* by Kapoor & Parker in Business Week, p. 91, 8 May 2000.
98. SCHULTZ, E. *Retirement Heist*, Portfolio/Penguin, New York 2011.
99. HUFFINGTON, A. *Pigs at the Trough*, Crown Publishers, New York 2003.

100. Special report: *Executive pay* by J. Reingold in Business Week, p. 100-142, 17 Apr 2000.
101. Article: *Steve Jobs an American disgrace* by Eric Alterman in The Nation, p. 9, 28 Nov 2011.
102. FREELAND, C. *Plutocrats*, Penguin Books, New York 2012.
103. LINDER, M. & I. NYGAARD *Void Where Prohibited*, Cornell U. Press, Ithaca, NY 1998.
104. Article: *Children's hour* by M. McLoughlin in U. S. News & World Report, p.34-40, 7 Nov 1988.
105. Article: *The next gun fight?* by Michael Scherer in TIME Magazine, p. 24-41, 28 Jan 2013.
106. Article: *Ten pro-gun claims that don't stand up* in Mother Jones, p. 56, Mar/Apr 2013.
107. Article: *Arms race* in TIME Magazine, p.14-15, 14 Jan 2013.
108. *One-fifth of America's children show signs of mental illness* , ABC TV - Evening News,19 Sep 2000.
109. FRANCES, A. *Saving Normal*, William Morrow, New York 2013.
110. PARKS, A. *An American Gulag*, The Education Exchange, Eldorado Springs, CO 2000.
111. MURRAY, C. *Coming Apart*, Crown Forum, New York 2012.
112. DOUTHAT, R. *Bad Religion*, Free Press, New York 2012.
113. *Psychological Warfare Manual*, CIA, U.S. Government, Washington 1985.
114. CARLE, G. L. *The Interrogator: An Education*, Nation Books, New York 2011.
115. *Kubark Counterintelligence Interrogation*, CIA Manual 1101, Washington 1963.
116. Article: *Meritocracy in America* in The Economist, p. 22-24, 1 Jan 2005.
117. Article: *Is America becoming more of a class society?* by Aaron Bernstein in Business Week, p. 86-91, 26 Feb 1996.
118. Article: *Whatever happened to upward mobility* by R. Foroohar in TIME Magazine, p. 26-34, 14 Nov 2011.
119 HUFFINGTON, A. *Third World America*, Crown Publishing Group, New York 2010.
120. UCHITELLE, L. *The Disposable American*, Vintage Books/Random House, New York 2006.
121. Article:*The nuclear waste problem* by M. Clayton in The Christian Science Monitor, 22 Mar 2010.
122. GOULD, J. M. & B. A. GOLDMAN *Deadly Deceit*, Four Walls Eight Windows, New York 1990.
123. Article: *Kingston fossil plant coal ash slurry spill* at www.wikipedia.org.
124. MOONEY, C. *The Republican War on Science*, Basic Books, New York 2005.
125. SOMOS *Tabula Rasa*, The Logos Foundation, Carson City, NV 1989.
126. McLUHAN, M. *Understanding Media*, McGraw-Hill, New York 1964.
127. TOFFLER, A. *Future Shock*, Bantam Books, New York 1970.
128. JUNG, C. G.*The Undiscovered Self*, Mentor Books, New York 1959.
129. FRANKYL, V. E. *Man's Search for Meaning*, Pocket Books, New York 1959.
130. WEINER, J. *The Next One Hundred Years*, Bantam Books, New York 1990.

Thomas E. Loxley

131. HEINBERG, R. *The Party's Over*, New Society Publishers, BC, Canada 2005.
132. Article: *The toxic waste trade with less industrialized countries* by Jennifer Clapp in Third World Quarterly, Vol. 15, No. 3, p. 505-518, 1994
133. WARD, B. *The Rich Nations and the Poor Nations*, W. W. Norton & Co, New York 1962.
134. JAMES, W.*The Varieties of Religious Experience*, Mentor Books, New York 1958.
135. ARMSTRONG, K. *A History of God*, Alfred A. Knopf, New York 1993.
136. WRIGHT, R. *The Evolution of God*, Back Bay Books, Little, Brown & Co, New York 2009.
137. DENNETT, D. *Breaking the Spell: Religion as a Natural Phenomenon*, Viking, New York 2006.
138. SARGENT, W. *Battle for the Mind*, Doubleday, New York 1957.
139. HOFFER, E. *The True Believer*, Harper & Row, New York 1951.
140. WALKER, W. *A History of the Christian Church*, Charles Scribner's Sons, New York 1945.
141. BEILBYED, J. K. *The Historical Jesus*, IVP Academic, Downers Grove, IL 2009.
142. KING, K.L. *The Gospel of Mary Magdala*, Polebridge Press, Santa Rosa, CA 2003.
143. DAVIES, S. *The Gospel of Thomas*, Skylight Paths Publishing, Woodstock, VT 2002.
144. HARRIS, S. *The End of Faith*, W. W. Norton & Co, New York 2004.
145. CROSSAN, J. D. *God and Empire*, Harper San Francisco/Harper Collins, New York 2007.
146. PHILLIPS, K. *American Theocracy*, Viking/Penguin Group, New York 2006.
147. SHARLET, J. *The Family* , Harper, New York 2008.
148. Article: *The end of the world - a brief history* in The Economist, p. 34-36, 18 Dec 2004.
149. LaHaye, T. & J. B. JENKINS *Left Behind* - Vol 12 *Glorius Appearing*, Tyndale House Publishers, Wheaton, IL 2004.
150. BIVINS, J. C. *Religion of Fear*, Oxford U. Press, New York 2008.
151. Article: *Second Coming Survey* by Hal Upchurch at www.tenderbytes.net/hal/2ndcoming.
152. GOLDSTEIN, R. *Betraying Spinoza*, Schocken Books, New York 2006.
153. ARMSTRONG, K. *The Battle for God* , Ballantine Books/Random House, New York 2001.
154. CLIFTON, R. J. *Super Power Syndrome*, Thunders Mouth Press, New York 2003.
155. HEDGES, C. *American Fascists*, Free Press, New York 2006.
156. BALK, A. *The Religion Business*, John Knox Press, Richmond, VA 1968.
157. *What country in the world has the most lawyers per capita* at www.wikianswers.com.
158. Article: *Food-disparagement laws: Oprah in trouble* in The Economist, 19 Jun 1997.
159. Article: *Food libel laws* at www.wikipedia.org.
160. Article: *Cheating Game* by C. Kleiner et al in U. S. News & World Report, p.55-66, 22 Nov 1999.
161. Article: *A nation of liars* by M. McLoughlin in U.S. News & World Report, p.54-60, 23 Feb 1987.
162. LEWIS, H. A. *Excellence Without a Soul*, Public Affairs/Perseus Books, Cambridge 2006.
163. PERKINS, J. *Confessions of an Economic Hit Man*, Berrett-Koehler, San Francisco 2004.
164. BLACK, E. *IBM and the Holocaust*, Crown Publishers, New York 2001.

165. Article: *The arms trade is big business* by Anup Shah at www.globalissues.org 23 Nov 2009.
166. Article: *The training schools* by Amnesty International USA at www.amnestyusa.org.
167. PIZZO, S. et al *Inside Job*, McGraw-Hill Publishing Co., New York 1989.
168. MANNING, R. D. *Credit Card Nation*, Basic Books, New York 2000.
169. SCHROTH, R. & A. L. ELLIOT *How Companies Lie*, Crown Business, New York, 2002
170. Article: *Reaganomics* at www.en.wikipedia.org.
171. AARONS, M. & J. LOFTUS *Secret War Against The Jews*, St. Martin's Press, New York 1994.
172. MICHAEL, R. *Concise History of American Antisemitism*, Rowman & Littlefield, Lanham 2005.
173. AARONS, M. & J. LOFTUS *Unholy Trinity*, St. Martin's Press, New York 1991.
174. Report: *War Crimes Committed Against U.S. Military Personnel June 8, 1967* by USS Liberty Veterans Assn 2005 at www.ussliberty.org.
175. EINSTEIN, A. *Letter to editor*, New York Times, 4 Dec 1948.
176. *Statistical Abstract of the United States: 2001*, U. S. Census Bureau, Washington, DC.
177. Article:*The myths and rewards of foreign aid* in U. S. News & World Report, p.9, 20 May 1996.
178. HEDGES, C. *Empire of Illusion*, Nation Books, New York 2009.
179. VIDAL, G. *Imperial Hubris*, Nation Books, New York 2004.
180. Article: *A U. S. victory, at a cost of $5.5-trillion* by Richard J. Newman in U.S. News & World Report, p. 38, 13 Jul 1998.
181. Briefing: *American power - the hobbled hegemon* in The Economist, p. 29-32, 30 Jun 2007.
182. WEINER, T. *Blank Check*: The Pentagon's Black Budget, Warner Books, New York 1990.
183. Article: *Monsanto's harvest of fear* by D. L. Barlett & J. B. Steele in Vanity Fair, May 2008.
184. HOFSTADTER, R. *The paranoid Style of American Politics*, Alfred A. Knopf, New York 1965.
185. STOUT, M. *The Sociopath Next Door*, Broadway Books, New York 2005.
186. CONASON, J. *It Can Happen Here*, St. Martin's Press, New York 2007.
187. ARCHER, J. *The Plot to Seize the White House*, Skyhorse Publishing, New York 2007
188. LAPHAM, L. H. *Pretensions to Empire*, The New Press, New York 2006.
189. DRURY, S. *Leo Strauss and the American Right*, St. Martin's, New York 1999.
190. NORTON, A. *Leo Strauss and the Politics of American Empire*, Yalebooks, New Haven 2004.
191. KLEIN, N. *The Shock Doctrine*, Metropolitan Books/Henry Holt & Co, New York 2007.
192. CARROLL, J. *House of War*, Houghton Mifflin Co., New York 2006.
193. SPREY, P. et al *The Pentagon Labyrinth* , Center for Defense Info, Washington 2011.
194. HIGGS, R. *Crisis and Leviathan*, p. 238, Oxford U. Press, New York 1987.

Thomas E. Loxley

195. WEINER, T. *Legacy of Ashes: The History of the CIA*, Doubleday, New York 2007.
196. KINZER, S. *Overthrow*, Times Books/Henry Holt & Co, New York 2006.
197. SHEEHAN, N. *The Pentagon Papers*, Quadrangle Books, New York 1971
198. SHEEHAN, N. *A Bright Shining Lie*, Random House, New York 1988.
199. MARCHETTI, V. & J. D. MARKS *CIA and the Cult of Intelligence*, Dell Pub Co, New York 1974.
200. TURSE, N. *Kill Anything That Moves*, Metropolitan Books, New York 2013.
201. CARROLL, M. C. *Lab 257*, William Morrow, New York 2004.
202. CALDICOTT, H. *The New Nuclear Danger*, The New Press, New York 2002.
203. JOHNSON, C. *Blowback*, Metropolitan Books, New York 2000.
204. TOYNBEE, A. J. *A Study of History*, Oxford U. Press, New York 1956.
205. FROMM, E. *Anatomy of Human Destructiveness*, Holt, Rinehart & Winston, New York 1973.
206. ATHENS, L. H. *The Creation of Dangerous Violent Criminals*, Routledge, New York 1989.
207. MORRIS, B. *1948*, Yale U. Press, New Haven 2008.
208. Article: *Rape, feces & urine-dipped cloth sacks* by W. Madsen in CounterPunch, 10 May 2004.
209. The following documented human rights abuses in Israel and the Occupied Territories:
    a. Breaking the Silence at www.breakingthesilence.org. Featured on Wikipedia.
    b. *Haaretz Newspaper* at www.haaretz.com.
    c. *American Friends Service Committee* at www.afsc.org.
    d. *The Association for Civil Rights in Israel* at www.acri.org.
    e. *Amnesty International* at www.amnesty.org.
    f. *Human Rights Watch* at www.hrw.org.
    g. *Rabbis for Human Rights Israel* at www.rhr.org.
    h. *Public Committee Against Torture in Israel* at www.stoptorture.org.il.
    i. *Israeli Information Center for Human Rights* at www.btselem.org.
210. Lexington: *No schmooze with the Jews* in The Economist, p. 31, 6-12 Apr 2002.
211. Article: *Shut up about the Jews already!* by Eric Alterman in The Nation, p. 9, 22 Oct 2012.
212. Article: *The Israel lobby* by Michael Lerner in TIKKUN, p. 33-83, Sep/Oct 2007.
213. MEARSCHEIMER, J. J. & S. M. WALT *The Israel Lobby and U. S. Foreign Policy*, Farrar, Strauss &Giroux, New York 2007.
214. BALL, G. W. & D. B. *The Passionate Attachment*, W. W. Norton & Co., New York 1992.
215. Article: *The cost of Israel to U. S. taxpayers* by Richard H. Curtiss in The Washington Report on Middle East Affairs 2006 at www.ifamericansknew.org.
216. Advertisement: *New anti-Semitism* by FLAME in U.S. News & World Report, p. 48, 9 Jan 2006.

217. Article: *Letter from Jerusalem* by David Remnick in <u>The New Yorker</u>, p. 32-37, 30 Jul 2007.
218. Article: *A brief history of ethnic cleansing* by A. Bell-Fialkoff in <u>Foreign Affairs</u>, p. 110-121, Summer 1993.
219. Article: *The clash of civilizations* by S. P. Huntington in <u>Foreign Affairs</u>, p. 22-49, Summer 1993.
220. Article: *The new global slave trade* by Ethan B. Kapstein in <u>Foreign Affairs</u>, p. 103-115, Nov/Dec 2006.
221. SAWYER, R. *Slavery in the Twentieth Century*, Routledge Kegan & Paul, London 1986.
222. CHOMSKY, N. *Hegemony or Survival*, Metropolitan Books/Henry Holt & Co, New York 2003.
223. LIEBER, J. B. *Rats in the Grain*, Four Walls Eight Windows Publishing, New York 2000.
224. Article: *Walmart's discounted ethics* by Rana Foroohar in <u>TIME Magazine</u>, p. 19, 7 May 2012.
225. ROBIN, M.-M. *The World According to Monsanto*, New Press, New York 2012.
226. JUDT, T. *Postwar: A History of Europe Since 1945*, Penguin Press, New York 2005.
227. FRANKLIN, H. B. *M. I. A. or Mythmaking in America*, Lawrence Hill Books, New York 1992.
228. MORRELL, D. *First Blood*, Warner Books, New York 1972.
229. Article: *Dick Cheney's song of America* by D. Armstrong in <u>Harper's Magazine</u>, p. 76-83, Oct 2002.
230. SUSKIND, R. *The One Percent Doctrine*, Simon & Schuster, New York 2006.
231. HERSH, S. M. *The Samson Option*, Random House, New York 1991.
232. PETERSON, P. P. *Running on Empty*, Farrar, Strauss& Giroux, New York 2004.
233. TAIBBI, M. *The Great Derangement*, Spiegel & Grau, New York 2008.
234. DEAN, J. W. *Broken Government*, Viking Adult, New York 2007.
235. NADER, R. *Cutting Corporate Welfare*, Seven Stories Press, New York 2000.
236. Article: *Great American pork barrel* by K. Silverstein in <u>Harper's Magazine</u>, p.31-38, Jul 2005.
237. CONTIETTI, M. *The K Street Gang*, Doubleday, New York 2006.
238. STONE, P. *Heist*, Farrar, Straus & Giroux, New York 2006.
239. Article: *Unaccountable:the high cost of the Pentagon's bad bookkeeping* by Scott J. Paltrow and Kelly Carr at <u>www.reuters.com</u> 2013.
240. Article: *The GOP war on voting* by Ari Berman in <u>Rolling Stone</u>, 15 Sep 2011.
241. PALAST, G. *Billionaires and Ballot Bandits*, Seven Stories Press, New York 2012.
242. FREEMAN, S. & J. BLEIFUSS *Was the 2004 Presidential Election Stolen?* Seven Stories Press, New York 2006.
243. Feature: *Theft of the 2000 presidential election* on <u>BBC-TV Newsnight</u>, 15 Feb 2001.

244. Article: *Coup de Tat* by David Henderson at www.angelfire.com.
245. MANN, T. & N. ORNSTEIN *It's Even Worse than it Looks*, Basic Books, New York 2012.
246. FROMM, E. *Escape From Freedom*, Discus Books/Published by Avon, New York 1941.
247. DOBBS, L. *War on the Middle Class*, Viking, New York 2006.
248. STIGLITZ, J. *The Price of Inequality*, W. W. Norton & Co, New York 2012.
249. KLINENBERG, E. *Fighting for Air*, Metropolitan Books, New York 2007.
250. BORJESSONED, K. *Into The Buzzsaw*, Prometheus Books, Amherst, NY 2004.
251. ELLISON, S. *War at the Wall Street Journal*, Houghton Mifflin Harcourt, New York 2010.
252. SCHECTER, D. *When News Lies*, Prometheus Books, Amherst, NY 2006.
253. PHILLIPS, K. *American Dynasty*, Viking, New York 2004.
254. MOORE, M. *Stupid White Men*, Regan Books, New York 2001.
255. WOODWARD, B. *State of Denial*, Simon & Schuster, New York 2006.
256. BACEVICH, A. J. *The New American Militarism*, Oxford U. Press, New York 2005.
257. Article: *How others see Americans* in The Economist, p. 35, 25 Jun 2005.
258. JOHNSON, C. *The Sorrows of Empire*, Metropolitan Books/Henry Holt & Co, New York 2004.
259. BARLETT, D. L. & J. STEELE *Critical Condition*, Doubleday, New York 2004.
260. Article: *America's health-care crisis* in The Economist, p. 24-26, 28 Jan/3 Feb 2006.
261. KOZOL, J. *The Shame of the Nation*, Crown Publishers, New York 2005.
262. BLACKMON, D. A. *Slavery by another Name*, Doubleday, New York 2008.
263. Article: *Taken* by Sarah Stillman in The New Yorker, p. 48-61, 12 & 19 Aug 2013
264. HARTUNG, W. *Prophets of War*, Nation Books, New York 2010.
265. Article: *Disposable Soldiers* by Joshua Korr in The Nation, p. 11-18, 26 Apr 2010.
266. CASHILL, J. & J. SANDERS *First Strike*, WND Books/Thomas Nelson Inc, Nashville, TN 2003.
267. Article: *The dark side of recruiting* by M. Thompson in TIME Magazine, p. 34-38, 13 Apr 2009.
268. Article: *AWOL in America* by Kathie Dobie in Harper's Magazine, p. 33-44, March 2005.
269. HERSH, S. M. *Chain of Command*, Harper Collins, New York 2004.
270. Article: *The war within* by Nancy Gibbs in TIME Magazine, p. 60, 8 Mar 2010.
271. HUNTER, M. *Honor Betrayed*, Barricade Books, Fort Lee, NJ 2007.
272. *Air Force Inspector General Summary Report Concerning The Handling of Sexual Assault Cases at the U. S. Air Force Academy*, Report to SECAF of 14 Sep 2004.
273. Article: *Christian emphasis on evangelism at heart of Air Force Academy scandal* by Steve Rabey in Religion News Service, 9 Jun 2005 at www.religionnews.com.
274. Article: *Rape statistics* at www.wikipedia.org/wiki/rape_statistics.
275. BROWNMILLER, S. *Against Our Will*, Bantam Books, New York 1975.
276. Article: *Sex and the superbug* by Jerome Groopman in The New Yorker, p. 26-30, 1 Oct 2012.

277. OMANG, J. *The CIAs Nicaragua Manual*, Vintage Books/Alfred A. Knopf, New York 1985.
278. Article: *George Bush and the CIA behind the assassination of prime minister Olof Palme* by John Anderson in Leopold Report, 1.519.942, 2003.
279. SEAGRAVE, S. *Gold Warriors*, Verso, New York 2003.
280. Article: *Classify this* by Graeme Wood in The Atlantic, p. 44-45, Sept 2007.
281. GUP, T. *Nation of Secrets*, Doubleday, New York 2007.
282. PRIEST, D. *Top Secret America*, Little, Brown & Co, New York 2011.
283. *Joint Army-Navy-Air Force Pub (JANAP) 146E* - Imposes $10,000 fine and 10-year prison sentence on personnel divulging any information on UFO sightings.
284. Article: *Project MKULTRA* at www.en.wikipedia.org.
285. MEERLOO, J.A.M. *The Rape of the Mind*, World Publishing Co, New York 1956.
286. RODGERS, J. E. *Psychosurgery*, Harper Collins, New York 1992.
287. BAMFORD, J. *The Shadow Factory*, Doubleday, New York 2008.
288. CARTER, G. *What We've Lost*, Farrar, Straus & Giroux, New York 2004.
289. NICHOLS, P. B. *The Montauk Project*, Sky Books, New York 1992.
290. KEELER, A. *Remote Mind Control Technology*, available on Internet.
291. BOWART, W. *Operation Mind Control*, St. Martin's Press, New York 1994.
292. *Apparatus for Treatment of Neuropsychic and Somatic Diseases* (Lida Machine) by L. Y. Rabichev et al, U.S. Patent 3773049.
293. *Electromagnetic Interaction with Biological Systems*, J. Lin ed, Plenum Press, New York 1989.
294. PERSINGER, M. *ELF and VLF Electromagnetic Field Effects*, Plenum Press, New York 1974.
295. Article: *U.S. military manpower crisis* by F. W. Kagan in Foreign Affairs, p. 97-110, Jul 2006.
296. FRANK, T. *What's the Matter With Kansas?*, Metropolitan Books, New York 2004.
297. STOCK, C. M. *Rural Radicals*, Cornell U. Press, Ithaca, NY 1996.
298. BRODEUR, P. *The Zapping of America*, W. W. Norton & Co, New York 1977.
299. *Rebuilding America's Defenses*, Project for a New American Century, Washington 2000.
300. *U.S. Public Law 107-56 USA PATRIOT Act* of 26 Oct 2001 (H.R. 3162).
301. SCARRY, E. *Rule of Law, Misrule of Men*, MIT Press, Boston 2010.
302. Article: *Acts of resistance* by Elaine Scarry in Harper's Magazine, p. 15-20, May 2004.
303. Article: *State of exception* by Scott Horton in Harper's Magazine, p. 74-81, July 2007.
304. *U.S. Public Law 109-364 or John Warner Defense Authorization Act of 2007* (H.R.5122-2)
305. De La VAGA, E. *U.S. v. George W. Bush et al*, Seven Stories Press, New York 2006.
306. BONIFAZ, J. C. *Warrior-King*, Nation Books, New York 2003.
307. *Articles of Impeachment Against George W. Bush* by Center for Constitutional Rights, Melville House Publishing at www.mhpbooks.com.

308. LOO, D. & P. PHILLIPS *Impeach the President*, Seven Stories Press, New York 2006.
309. U. S. Representative Dennis Kucinich, Democrat of Ohio, offered *35 Count Resolution to Impeach George W. Bush* in Congressional Record of 9 Jun 2008.
310. SANDS, P. *Lawless World*, Viking, New York 2005.
311. HOFF, J. *A Faustian Foreign Policy*, Cambridge U. Press, New York 2008.
312. BUGLIOSI, V. *Prosecution of George W. Bush for Murder*, Vanguard, Cambridge, MA 2008.
313. STIGLITZ, J. E. & L. J. BILMES *Three Trillion Dollar War*, W. W. Norton & Co, New York 2008.
314. Article: *Iraq war facts, 31 Jan 2012* by Deborah White at www.usliberals.about.com.
315. CARTER, G. *What We've Lost*, Farrar, Straus and Giroux, New York 2004.
316. Article: *Shifting targets* by Seymour Hersh in The New Yorker, p. 40-47, 8 Oct 2007.
317. Article: *Letter from Tel Aviv* by David Remnick in The New Yorker, p. 22-28, 8 Sep 2012.
318. CHATTERJEE, P. *Iraq Inc.*, Seven Stories Press, New York 2004.
319. St. CLAIR, J. *Grand Theft Pentagon*, Common Courage Press, Monroe, ME 2005.
320. Article: *Contract with America* by Daphne Eviatar in Harper's Magazine, p. 74-77, Oct 2007.
321. CLARK, W. R. *Petrodollar Warfare*, New Society Publishers, British Columbia, Canada 2005.
322. Article: *14 enduring bases set in Iraq* by Christine Spolar in Chicago Tribune, 23 Mar 2004.
323. In 1986 the U.S. Nuclear Control Institute admitted that 9600 pounds of 'bomb grade' uranium and plutonium was missing in the U.S., enough to build 200 Hiroshima bombs.
324. SMITH, A. *The Theory of Moral Sentiments*, Cosimo Classics, New York 1759.
325. De SOTO, H. *The Mystery of Capital*, Basic Books, New York 2000.
326. FRANKEN, A. *Lies and the Lying Liars that Tell Them*, Dutton, New York 2003.
327. MOONEY, C. *The Republican Brain*, Wiley, New York 2012.
328. BROCK, D. & A. RABIN-HAVT *The Fox Effect*, Anchor Books/Random House, New York 2012.
329. PRESS, B. *The Obama Hate Machine*, Thomas Dunne Books, New York 2012.
330. WELCH, B. *State of Confusion*, Thomas Dunne Books, New York 2008.
331. FRANK, T. *The Wrecking Crew*, Metropolitan Books/Henry Holt & Co, New York 2008.
332. BAZELON, E. *Sticks and Stones*, Random House, New York 2013.
333. OLWEUS, D. *Bullying at School*, Blackwell Publishing, Malden, MA 1993.
334. BAKER, R. *Family of Secrets*, Bloomsbury Press, New York 2009.
335. SKOCPOL, T. & V. WILLIAMSON *The Tea Party and the Remaking of Republican Conservatism*, Oxford U. Press, New York 2012.
336. Article: *Covert operations* by Jane Mayer in The New Yorker, p. 44-55, 30 Aug 2010.

337. Article: *Money unlimited* by Jeffrey Toobin in The New Yorker, p. 36-47, 21 May 2012.
338. HEDGES, C. *Death of the Liberal Class*, Nation Books, New York 2010.
339. EDWARDS, M. *The Parties versus The People*, Yale U. Press, New Haven, CT 2012.
340. In March 2006 the U.S. Federal Reserve halted report of the M3 money supply, key measure used by European Central Bank and others to evaluate the currency.
341. McDONALD, F. *The Phaeton Ride*, Doubleday & Co, Garden City, NY 1974.
342. NAYLOR, R. T. *Hot Money and the Politics of Debt*, Linders Press, New York 1989.
343. POLANYI, K. *The Great Transformation*, Beacon Press, Boston 2001.
344. MINSKY, H. P. *Stabilizing an Unstable Economy*, McGraw-Hill, New York 2008.
345. SORKIN, A. R. *Too big to Fail*, Viking, New York 2009.
346. REINHART, C. M. & K. S. ROGOFF *This Time is Different*, Princeton U. Press 2009.
347. SCHEER, R. *The Great American Stickup*, Nation Books, New York 2010.
348. JOHNSON, S. & J. KWAK *13 Bankers*, Pantheon Books, New York 2010.
349. LEWIS, M. *The Big Short*, W. W. Norton & Co, New York 2010.
350. McLEAN B. & J. NOCERA *All the Devils are Here*, Portfolio/Penguin, New York 2010.
351. TETT, G. *Fool's Gold*, The Free Press, New York 2010.
352. MORGENSON, G. & J. ROSNER *Reckless Endangerment*, Times Books, New York 2011.
353. SMITH, G. *Why I Left Goldman Sachs*, Grand Central Publishing, New York 2012.
354. ONARAN, Y. *Zombie Banks*, Bloomberg Press/Wiley, Hoboken, NJ 2012.
355. DOYLE, L. *In Bed with Wall Street*, Palgrave Macmillan, New York 2014.
356. ALPEROVITZ, G. *America Beyond Capitalism*, John Wiley & Sons, Hoboken 2011.
357. Article: *What would Keynes do?*, by Thomas Geoghegan in The Nation, p. 11-17, 17 Oct 2011.
358. KRUGMAN, P. *End This Depression Now*, W. W. Norton & Co, New York 2012.
359. BAIR, S. *Bull by the Horns*, Free Press, New York 2012.
360. REICH, R. B. *Beyond Outrage*, Alfred A. Knopf, New York 2012.
361. BARTLETT, B. *The Benefit and the Burden*, Simon & Schuster, New York 2012.
362. EDELMAN, P. *So Rich, So Poor*, New Press, New York 2012.
363. Article: *Hey, Washington* by G. Colvin & A. Sloan in Fortune, p. 82-91, 3 Sep 2012.
364. Article: *Death by a thousand cuts* by Kevin Drum in Mother Jones, p. 16-67, Sep/Oct 2013.
365. WIEDEMER, D. et al *Aftershock*, John Wiley & Sons, Hoboken, NJ 2011.
366. Article: *How Wall St. is still rigging the game* by G. Smith in TIME Magazine, p. 18, 5 Nov 2012.
367. Article: *The secret sharer* by Jane Mayer in The New Yorker, p. 47-57, 23 May 2011.
368. Article: *NSA is building biggest spy center* by J. Bamford in Wired Magazine, 15 Mar 2012.

Thomas E. Loxley

369. ENGELHART, T. *The United States of Fear*, Haymarket Books, Chicago 2011.
370. SUSKIND, R. *Confidence Men*, Harper Collins, New York 2011.
371. SANGER, D. *Confront and Conceal*, Crown, New York 2012.
372. Article: *The lethal presidency of Barack Obama* by Tom Junod in Esquire Magazine, 9 Jul 2012.
373. BENJAMIN, M. *Drone Warfare*, OR Books 2012 via www.orbooks.com.
374. Article: *The untold story-Obama's crackdown on whistleblowers* by Tim Shorrock in The Nation, p. 11-18, 15 Apr 2013.
375. SIFRY, M. *WikiLeaks and the Age of Transparency*, Counterpoint, Berkeley 2010.
376. LEIGH, D. *WikiLeaks*, Public Affairs, New York 2011.
377. ALTERMAN, E. *When Presidents Lie*, Viking Adult, New York 2004.
378. VENTURA, J. *63 Documents the Gov'mt Doesn't Want You to Read*, Skyhorse, New York 2011.
379. NAPOLITANO, A. P. *Lies the Government Told You*, Thomas Nelson, Nashville, TN 2010.
380. SOUTHWELL, D. *Secrets and Lies*, Carlton Publishing, London 2005.
381. HESSEL, S. *Time for Outrage!* Twelve/Hachette Book Group, New York 2010.
382. UNGER, D. C. *The Emergency State*, Penguin Press, New York 2012.
383. JOHNSON, C. *Dismantling the Empire*, Metropolitan Books, New York 2010.
384. GARRISON, J.A. *America as Empire*, Berrett-Koehler, San Francisco 2004
385. MANDER, J. *In the Absence of the Sacred*, Sierra Club Books, Washington 1992.
386. BAKAN, J. *The Corporation*, The Free Press, New York 2004.
387. COLL, S. *Private Empire*, Penguin Press, New York 2012.
388. Article: *NAFTA on steroids* by Lori Wallach in The Nation, 27 Jun 2012.
389. KOSMAN, J. *The Buyout of America*, Portfolio/Penguin, New York 2010.
390. LESSIG, L. *Republic, Lost*, Twelve, New York 2011.
391. JOHNSON, C. *Nemesis*, Metropolitan Books, New York 2006.
392. ROTHKOPF, D. *Power, Inc.*, Farrar, Straus & Giroux, New York 2012.
393. WOLIN, S. *Democracy Incorporated*, Princeton U. Press, Princeton, NJ 2008.
394. DeVILLIERS, M. *The End*, Thomas Dunne Books/St. Martin's Press, New York 2008.
395. GOODMAN, A. & D. MOYNIHAN *The Silenced Majority*, Haymarket Books, Chicago 2012.
396. HARTMANN, T. *The Crash of 2016*, Twelve, New York 2013.
397. Article: *Instant Runoff Voting* by Center for Voting & Democracy at www.fairvote.org.
398. FERGUSON, N. *The Great Degeneration*, Penguin Press, New York 2013.
399. RIFKIN, I. *Spiritual Perspectives on Globalization*, Skylight Paths, Woodstock, VT 2003
400. SAUL, J. R. *The collapse of Globalism*, Viking, New York 2005.

ABOUT THE AUTHOR

Thomas Loxley is a 1961 graduate of the innovative engineering science R&D program at Case Institute of Technology. He studied thermodynamics under Dr. Jerzy Moszynski, a noted authority on multiple heat source systems. He is a former Navy scientist and Virginia Tech professor listed in American Men of Science and classified as Mechanical Engineer, General Engineer and Physicist by the U.S. Civil Service. He coauthored the *U.S. Energy Policy Game* and led Virginia energy conservation. His inverted cave research into tapping the solar energy stored in the Earth's surface involved active membership in International Council for Building Research Studies and Documentation (CIB) and its W67 Working Commission on Energy Conservation in the Built Environment. W67 papers were published in Sweden in 87, Austria in 88, France in 89, Germany in 90, and Norway in 91. Others were published in CIB World Congress Proceedings in Washington in 86 and Paris in 89, CIB Journal in 85 and 92, plus the National Bureau of Standards (now NIST) in 81, U.S. Solar Energy Society in 82, Sweden's North Sun Conference in 88, UK World Renewable Energy Congress in 90, and IEA World Conference in Canada in 93. Other work has included investigating Vietnam weapon failures, longwall mine roof supports, inventing test instrumentation, eliminating major shipboard hazard, helping build Pisces deep-diving submersibles. Selected for Peace Corps, elected precinct Judge of Elections. Has traveled extensively, hiking Austria and Ireland. Survived open heart surgery, COVID, etc. Recent books include *Align Your Minds,* promoting self-improvement, and the essays *Our Global Warming Legacy* and *America's Manifest Destiny.* He is now finalizing major handbook on his inverted cave research. Inactive on social media, he lives on the Ohio River in Beaver, PA

GLOBAL WARMING REALITY
A Naturalist Action Plan
Thomas E. Loxley

Global warming is a result of Earth's solar absorption exceeding its ability to dissipate that heat into space. Some exploitive politicians want you to think this is all a simple matter of excess atmospheric greenhouse gases suppressing the Earth's heat dissipation rate. While some regional production of greenhouse gases have slightly declined, the overall release of both CO_2 and methane have been steadily increasing. Moreover, no effort to speed up its dissipation can succeed as long as the absorption rate is constantly growing due to our expanding human population, with all of the land development and energy consumption it entails. This process seems tailor made to soak up ever more solar radiation. The outer twenty meters (66 ft) of the Earth's surface constitutes one huge solar collector. Modern industry created global warming by wantonly destroying the vital insulative effect provided by the enormous forest canopy that had once shielded much of the Earth's surface from the Sun's direct radiation. We are now irresponsibly driving many of Earth's most magnificent lifeforms rapidly into extinction. The very survival of human civilization now depends upon our working together to immediately increase the solar reflectivity of the planet's surface in order to buy the time needed to restore the forest canopy we destroyed.

Available on Internet

Expanded Third Edition

ALIGN YOUR MINDS
Seize YOUR Dream
- Your Guide To Using Your Inner Mind -

Thomas E. Loxley

You can do it! Let your inner mind keep your eyes fixed firmly on the prize. We all have two minds, one that's conscious and one subconscious. Properly reviewing your own personal objectives, just before going to sleep, you can activate your subconscious mind to focus your mental and emotional energy on achieving just what you want to do. While exploiters are now psychologically manipulating everybody to serve their interests, autosuggestion can really help you to take control of your personal destiny. It is the most powerful tool ever known for self improvement. Realizing its full potential now requires that you understand how your two minds work, how they react to what's happening around you, how you can best influence your subconscious mind, and how you might explore your own subconscious perspective. The objective is to help you to know yourself and the full realization of your own personal potential. Let *ALIGN YOUR MINDS* now show you how you might use your inner mind to help you to get ahead.

Available on Internet

THE U.S. ENERGY POLICY GAME

The U.S. Department of Energy introduced Citizen's Workshops on Energy and the Environment in the 1970s. The outreach programs were designed to help people understand the ongoing energy crisis. It used an interactive type of computer, called the Energy Environment Simulator, that had incorporated an electronic display showing how various social and industrial decisions might affect America's future. It allowed diverse groups to explore the effects of altering the population growth, lifestyle, and energy sources, to systematically explore these various concerns and their social ramifications. It promoted an informed democratic debate among the diverse players on these matters. However, its awkwardness, complexity, and cost tended to limit its utilization.

At Virginia Tech, the author and physicist, Dr. Samuel P. Bowen, teamed up to create the 'U.S. Energy Policy Game' in 1977. This was a simple exercise using an instructional booklet, circular slide-rule type calculator, and data tabulation forms. Like the DOE computer, the objective was to help people visualize various policy issues, and the time required to change the nature of our society. It allowed individuals and groups to explore the effects of various national strategies, and helped them to understand what community action might be required to produce the desired results. The Policy Effects calculator allowed the players to consider alterations of the nation's population growth, energy demand, and key resources, including coal, oil, natural gas, nuclear, and renewable energy. Given an initial national population and lifestyle, the total energy demand was first determined. The next step explored the mix of production facilities that might best meet that requirement. This helped players to appreciate the powerful role played by their personal energy conservation. The booklet showed how to use the computer, and provided a background discussion of the various issues involved, providing the latest estimates of the domestic and global resources available. The players were challenged to design policies that would allow those resources to last the longest, while still providing the population with a satisfactory sort of lifestyle.

Although the game was created to serve the population in Virginia, it proved popular with schools around the country. It was praised by DOE, the National 4-H council, and National Science Teachers Association (NSTA). NSTA subsequently developed a similar game of their own. A modern improvement of our 1977 game, using smartphones, is currently envisioned to make it suitable for even younger children and most any country in the world.

www.ingramcontent.com/pod-product-compliance
Lightning Source LLC
Chambersburg PA
CBHW070549030426
42337CB00016B/2414